Hugo Pinksterboer

Tipbook
Violin and
Viola

Handy, clearly written, and up-to-date.
The reference manual for both beginning and advanced
violinists, including Tipcodes and a glossary.

THE **TIPBOOK**
COMPANY

THE BEST GUIDE TO YOUR INSTRUMENT!

Thanks

For their information, their expertise, their time, and their help we'd like to thank the following musicians, teachers, technicians, and other violin experts: Isabelle van Keulen, Nello Mirando, Theo Olof, Edward C. Campbell (violin maker, PA), David Rivinus (violin maker, OR), Duane Lightner (Discount String Center, IN), Kim Rodney and Frederik Habel (Gewa, Germany), Lang Shen (Knilling String Instruments, MO), Heinz Kovacs (Thomastik-Infeld, Austria), Sandy Neill (D'Addario, NY), Volker Müller-Zierach (Pirastro, Germany), Klaus Clement (Höfner, Germany), Barbara Van Itallie (Violin Society of America), Levent Aslan, Mies Albarda (European String Teachers Association (ESTA/ARCO), Jaap Bolink (violin maker), Taner Erkek, Harm van der Geest, Hilka Jelsma, Siard de Jong, Fred Lindeman (violin maker), Hans and Sonja Neuburger, Annelies Steinhauer (violin maker), Eduard van Tongeren (violin maker), Tom van Berkel, Bas van den Broek, Guust François (violin maker), Andreas Grütter (bow maker), Eric Matser, A.L. Matser, Marja Mosk, Fred Pinksterboer, Irmela Schlingensiepen (violin maker), Helena and Jelle van Tongeren, and Harry Vogel. The violin on the cover is played by Bregje van Tongeren.

Anything missing?

Any omissions? Any areas that could be improved? Please go to www.tipbook.com to contact us; thanks!

The makers

Journalist, writer, and musician **Hugo Pinksterboer**, author of *The Tipbook Series*, has published hundreds of interviews and articles, as well as instrument, video, CD, and book reviews for national and international music magazines.

Illustrator, designer, and musician **Gijs Bierenbroodspot** has worked as an art director for a wide variety of magazines and has developed numerous ad campaigns. While searching in vain for information about saxophone mouthpieces, he got the idea for this series of books on music and musical instruments. He is responsible for the layout and illustrations for all of the Tipbooks.

Acknowledgements

Concept, design, and illustrations: Gijs Bierenbroodspot
Cover photo: René Vervloet
Translation: MdJ Copy & Translation
Editor: Robert L. Doerschuk
Proofreaders: Nancy Bishop, Patricia Waddy

Tipbook Violin and Viola

Publishing Details

This second edition published Februari 2005 by
The Tipbook Company bv, The Netherlands.

Distributed exclusively by the Hal Leonard Corporation,
7777 West Bluemound Road, P.O. Box 13819,
Milwaukee, Wisconsin 53213.

Typeset in Glasgow and Minion.

Printed in The Netherlands by Hentenaar Boek bv, Nieuwegein.

144pp

ISBN 90-76192-39-1

IN BRIEF

Have you just started playing? Are you thinking about buying a violin or viola? Or do you want to find out more about the instrument you already have? If so, this book will tell you everything you need to know. About buying or renting an instrument, about tailpieces, bridges and fingerboards, about bows, strings, and tuning. About the best way to maintain your instrument, about the history of the violin, about its family, and much, much more.

The best you can

Having read this Tipbook, you'll be able to get the most out of your instrument, to buy the best violin or viola you can, and to easily grasp any other literature on the subject, from magazines to books and Internet publications.

The first four chapters

If you have just started playing, or haven't yet begun, pay particular attention to the first four chapters. Have you been playing longer? Then skip ahead to Chapter 5.

Please note that all prices mentioned in this book reflect only approximate street prices in US dollars. As a rule, all references to violins and violinists in this book apply to violas and violists as well.

Glossary

Most of the violin terms you'll come across in this book are briefly explained in the glossary at the end. To make life even easier, it doubles as an index.

Hugo Pinksterboer

CONTENTS

VIII SEE WHAT YOU READ WITH TIPCODE
www.tipbook.com
The Tipcodes in this book give you access to additional
information (short movies, soundtracks, photos, etc.)
at www.tipbook.com. Here's how it works.

1 CHAPTER 1. VIOLINISTS AND VIOLISTS
As a violinist or violist you can play in small
ensembles and large orchestras, and you can play a
wide variety of styles, from classical to rock and folk.

5 CHAPTER 2. A QUICK TOUR
The instrument in bird's-eye view, and the main
differences between violins and violas.

14 CHAPTER 3. LEARNING TO PLAY
A chapter about violin lessons and practicing.

19 CHAPTER 4. BUYING OR RENTING
Especially if you're young, it may be advisable to rent
a violin rather than to buy one. If you are going to
buy one, here is roughly what it will cost.

26 CHAPTER 5. A GOOD VIOLIN
Tips for comparing and play-testing violins, so that
you can choose the best possible instrument.

48 CHAPTER 6. GOOD STRINGS
All about different strings: core materials, windings,
sound, and much more.

57 CHAPTER 7. BOWS AND ROSINS
A guide to choosing bows and an introduction to the
many types of rosin.

68 CHAPTER 8. FITTINGS, MUTES, AND CASES
Choosing chin rests and shoulder rests is made easier
with the information in this chapter, which also
deals with other accessories, such as mutes and cases.

80   CHAPTER 9. ELECTRIC VIOLINS
A guide to electric violins, and how to turn your instrument into an electric one.

85   CHAPTER 10. TUNING
About tuning, fine tuners, tuning forks, electronic tuners, and more.

91   CHAPTER 11. VIOLIN MAINTENANCE
All about what you can do to keep your violin, your strings, and your bow in good condition, and what you'd better leave to a violin maker or technician.

108   CHAPTER 12. BACK IN TIME
A lot of history in a few words.

111   CHAPTER 13. THE FAMILY
The violin has quite a few relatives, as well as a whole lot of acquaintances.

114   CHAPTER 14. HOW THEY'RE MADE
An introduction to the basics of violin making.

118   CHAPTER 15. VIOLIN BRANDS AND MAKERS
Some of the main names in violin making, old and new.

122   GLOSSARY AND INDEX
What is a saddle, where would you find the bass bar, and what is purfling for? This glossary doubles as an index, so you can use it as a handy reference section.

128   TIPCODE LIST
All violin Tipcodes listed.

129   WANT TO KNOW MORE?
Still curious? Information about magazines, books, and the Internet, and about the makers of this book.

132   ESSENTIAL DATA
Two pages to list the essential information about your instrument and strings.

SEE AND HEAR WHAT YOU READ WITH TIPCODE

www.tipbook.com

In addition to the many illustrations on the following pages, Tipbooks offer you a new way to see—and even hear—what you are reading about. The Tipcodes that you will come across throughout this book give you access to short videos, sound files, and other additional information at www.tipbook.com.

How it works is very simple. One example: On page 87 of this book you can read about using fine tuners. Right above that paragraph it says **Tipcode 006**.

Type in that code on the Tipcode page at www.tipbook.com and you will see a short movie that shows you how to use them.

Enter code, watch movie
You enter the Tipcode beneath the movie window on the Tipcode page. In most cases, you will then see the relevant images within five to ten seconds. Tipcodes activate a short video, sound, or both, or a series of photos.

Tipcodes listed
For your convenience, the Tipcodes presented in this book are shown in a single list on page 128.

Quick start
The Tipcode videos, pictures, and sound files are designed to start quickly. If you miss something the first time, you can of course repeat them as often as you like. And if it all happens too fast, use the pause button below the movie window.

First, make your selection: Tipcode, chords and fingering charts, or the glossary.

The Tipcode window displays movies, photo series, fingering charts, chords, and explanations of the words used in this book.

Enter a Tipcode here and click on the button. Want to see it again? Click again.

These buttons and links take you directly to other interesting sites.

Plug-ins

If the software plug-ins you need to view the videos are not yet installed on your computer, you'll automatically be told what you need, and where you can download it. This kind of software is free.

Still more at www.tipbook.com

You can find even more information at www.tipbook.com. For example, you can look up words in the glossaries of *all* the Tipbooks. There are chord diagrams for guitarists and pianists; fingering charts for saxophonists, clarinetists, and flutists; and rudiments for drummers. Also included are links to some of the websites mentioned in the *Want to Know More?* section of each Tipbook.

1. VIOLINISTS AND VIOLISTS

Practicing the violin is something you usually do alone. Performing, on the other hand, you'll usually do with others. In an orchestra, with twenty or thirty other violinists, or in a string quartet with two violins, a viola, and a cello. Or in a band, perhaps playing jazz or folk. A chapter about all the things you can do with a violin, about violinists, and about what makes it so much fun.

Violins and violas are *string instruments*. You play them by drawing a bow across the strings. That's why they're also known as *bowed instruments*.

Bigger and lower   Tipcode VIOLIN-001
The viola looks just the same as the violin. The main difference is that it is bigger. As a result, it sounds a little lower.

All kinds of styles   Tipcode VIOLIN-002
Most violinists play classical music, but you'll find them in many other styles too—in folk music from many different countries, in gypsy music and Jewish klezmer, in tango and Turkish music, but also in the blues, in Cajun, country, and jazz. In the late 1990s Vanessa Mae even made the charts, playing an electric violin.

Classical
There is a wide variety of classical violin music available. That's not surprising, because the instrument has been around for four centuries. All in all there is so much violin music that you couldn't play it in a lifetime.

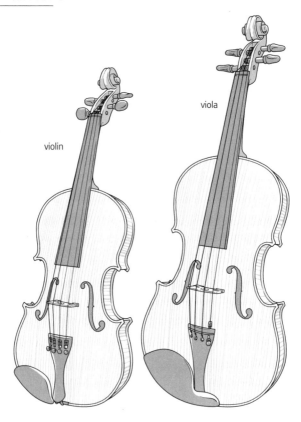

A viola is slightly bigger than a violin.

Small and large

Classical music can be played in large and small orchestras, in quartets, and in many other kinds of groups and ensembles. Here are some examples.

Symphony orchestra

The violin is the main voice of the largest orchestra of all, the symphony orchestra, with some fifty or more members. Besides the violin and the viola, a symphony orchestra includes the two much larger string instruments as well: the *cello*, held between the legs of the cellist, and the *double bass*, which is so large that the musician sits on a high stool.

Other instruments

Besides the *strings* (violin, viola, cello, double bass) you'll find all kinds of other instruments in the symphony orchestra, such as brasswinds (trumpet, French horn, trombone, etc.), woodwinds (clarinet, flute, oboe, bassoon and so on), percussion instruments (snare drums, tympani, cymbals), a harp, a grand piano…

More than thirty

Violins aren't very loud, but they're very important to the sound of a symphony orchestra. That's why there are more of them than any other instrument. A typical orchestra may have sixteen violinists, and some even have more than thirty.

First and second violins

The violinists are always divided into two groups: the first and second violinists. You could think of the first violinists as the singer of the band: They often play the melody that you go on humming to yourself after a concert. The second violinists, who are equally important, usually accompany the melody.

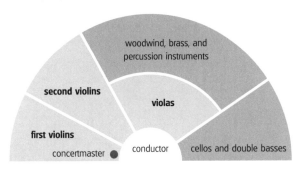

An example of the arrangement of the instruments in a symphony orchestra. The violins are always at the front.

The violists

The viola players, also known as *violists*, have their own role. The different string sections are not unlike the different groups of singers in a choir. A large orchestra may have sixteen violists.

Concertmasters

The strings are always at the front, around the conductor. To the conductor's left, right at the front, is the concertmaster, who is the leader of all the musicians in the orchestra. The second violins and the violas each have their own leaders as well; they're the principal second violinist and the principal violist. The louder instruments, such as the trumpets and percussion instruments, are further toward the back.

String quartet

A lot of classical music has been written for smaller groups too. A well-known and very popular ensemble is the string quartet, for instance, with two violinists, a violist and a cellist.

Duo and solo

There is also a lot of music for duos—a violinist and a pianist, for example. There are even pieces that are meant to be played solo—just a violin, and nothing else. Of course, that's a different type of solo playing than when you play 'solo' violin accompanied by a full orchestra.

A few bars from a string quartet (W. A. Mozart); music for two violins, viola, and cello.

Violin or viola?

Many violists started out on a violin—only later did they discover that they preferred the lower, warmer sound of a viola. Of course, you can also start on a viola. If you make the switch later, the viola will take a bit of getting used to.

2. A QUICK TOUR

A violin has a body, a neck and a fingerboard, four strings, four pegs, and a whole list of other parts. A chapter about what everything's called, what it's for and where to find it, about the differences between violins and violas, and about violins for children.

The violin you see on the next page looks remarkably like a violin made a hundred or more years ago. A viola is bigger; that's the most important difference. Violins and violas made specially for children's hands are also available (see pages 12–13).

Body
The main part of the violin, the *body*, is the soundbox of the instrument: It amplifies the sound of the strings.

Top and back
The *top* and the *back* of the body are noticeably arched. The top, with two *f*-shaped *soundholes* or *f-holes*, is most important for the sound of the instrument.

Tuning pegs
You tune the strings using the *pegs* or *tuning pegs*. There is one peg for each string, at the top of the violin, fitted in the *pegbox*.

Scroll
Right at the top is the *scroll* or *volute*. Some violins have the head of a lion, a woman, or an angel instead of a regular scroll.

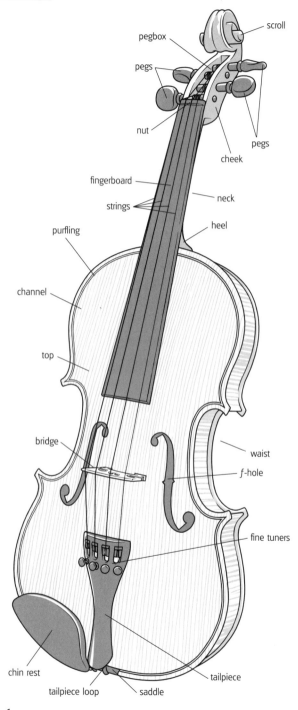

scroll

pegbox

pegs

nut

pegs

cheek

fingerboard

neck

strings

purfling

heel

channel

top

bridge

waist

f-hole

fine tuners

chin rest

tailpiece

tailpiece loop

saddle

Fingerboard

The strings run along the *fingerboard*. To make the strings produce higher notes, you *stop* them by pressing them onto the fingerboard. Stopping a string makes the section that vibrates shorter. As a result, it will sound higher.

The neck

The fingerboard is a thin, dark plank that's glued to the *neck*. The neck runs from the scroll to the body. The fingerboard is quite a bit longer: A large part juts out over the body.

Nut

At the top of the fingerboard, the strings run over a small ridge called the *nut*.

The bridge

About halfway down the body, the strings run over the *bridge*, a small piece of wood that's much lighter in color than the rest of the violin.

When you play, you're actually making the strings vibrate with your bow. The bridge passes on those vibrations to the top. This makes sure the instrument will be heard: The top, together with the rest of the body, amplifies the sound.

Rounded bridge

The bridge is rounded, just like the top of the fingerboard. This allows you to bow the two middle strings without touching the outer strings.

Feet

The bridge stands on the top on its two *feet*, without the help of glue or screws. The pressure of the strings is enough to make sure it doesn't fall over.

Tailpiece and fine tuners

The strings are attached to the pegs at one end and to the *tailpiece* at the other. Inside the tailpiece there are usually one or more *fine tuners*, which allow you to tune your violin more easily than with the big wooden tuning pegs.

Tailpiece loop, end button, and saddle

The tailpiece is attached to the (*end*) *button* with a loop known as the *tailpiece loop*. To make sure this loop doesn't damage the body, it runs over the *saddle* or *bottom nut*.

Under your chin...
Near the tailpiece you'll also find the *chin rest*. Because there are as many different chins as there are people, chin rests come in all shapes and sizes.

... and on your shoulder
On the other side, against the back of the violin, is a *shoulder rest*, or sometimes simply a cushion. This makes the violin sit a little higher up your shoulder. Even so, violinists still need to tilt their heads to the left a little when they play. The shoulder rest, chin rest, tailpiece, pegs, and end button are collectively known as the *fittings* or the *trim*.

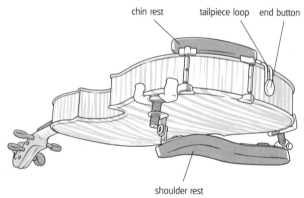

chin rest   tailpiece loop   end button

shoulder rest

Purfling
The inlaid *purfling* runs along the edge of the body. It is usually made of three strips of wood—two ebony or dark dyed strips, and a lighter wood in between.

Channel
From the edge, the top usually dips a little, before the upward arching begins. This 'valley' is called the *channel*. The back has almost the same shape.

Heel and shoulder
The semicircular part that sticks out at the top of the back is called the *heel*. The shoulder, the wider bottom part of the neck that links it to the body, is glued to that heel.

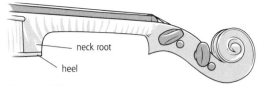

neck root

heel

Violin or viola?

When you first compare a violin to a viola, the overall size may be the only difference you see—but there is more. Violas are not only a bit wider and taller, but they're slightly deeper too; the sides of the body or *ribs* are higher. A detail: Some violas have a kind of 'step' near the pegbox.

Lower and darker

As a result of its larger dimensions, a viola sounds not only lower, but also a bit darker and fuller than a violin—more than what the pitch difference alone would suggest.

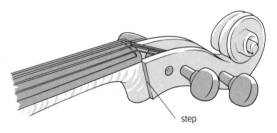

step

You can sometimes tell a viola by this 'step.'

INSIDE

There is plenty to see inside a violin too, from the sound post to the bass bar, the maker's label, and a number of small wooden blocks.

The sound post

If you look through the *f*-hole at the treble side of the instrument (by the thinnest string), you can just about see a length of round wood, wedged between the top and the back. That's the *sound post*. Without it, violins and violas would sound very thin or hollow.

The bass bar

Near the other *f*-hole, on the bass side, is the *bass bar*. This strengthens the top and enhances the lower frequencies of the instrument.

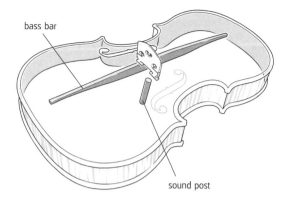

bass bar

sound post

The bass bar and sound post are important to the sound of a violin.

The label
You'll be able to see only a tiny bit of the bass bar, by looking from the side and through the top part of the f-hole. If you look straight down through the same hole, you may see the maker's label.

THE BOW
To play your violin you need a bow, which is almost as important as the instrument itself.

Bow hair and stick
The bow hair—some hundred and fifty hairs—almost always come from a horse's tail. One end of the hair is held in place inside the *head* or *tip*, at the top end of the *stick* or *bow stick*. The other end is held in place inside the *frog*.

Tension
Before you play, you have to tension the hair: Turn the *screw button* clockwise until there's about 0.25" (5–6 mm) between the hair and the middle of the stick. After you have finished playing, turn the screw button counterclockwise until the hair goes slack. The screw button is also known as *end screw* or *adjuster*.

Bow grip
You hold the bow at the (*bow*) *grip*, often made of leather, and the *winding*, usually of very thin metal wire. Apart from enhancing your grip, this also protects the wood.

Rosin

For the bow to do its job properly, you need to rub the hair with a piece of violin *rosin*. This makes the hair slightly sticky. Without rosin, the bow will slide across the strings without producing a sound.

STRINGS AND CLEFS

Both the violin and the viola have four strings, which come in steel, gut or synthetic versions. The thicker strings are usually wound with ultra-thin metal wire.

Violin: G, D, A, E

The four violin strings are tuned to the notes G, D, A, and E, as shown on the piano keyboard on the next page. The G is the lowest sounding string; the thin E the highest.

Viola: C, G, D, A

The first illustration on the next page also shows the notes of the viola strings. The thickest, lowest sounding string produces a C. The other three viola strings are tuned to the same pitches as the three lowest violin strings: G, D, and A.

Violin music on paper

Violin music is written in a staff that begins with the *G clef*, also known as the *treble clef*. The tail of this curly symbol circles the second line from below, indicating the note G. This G sounds an octave higher than the lowest note you can play on a violin.

The viola key

When using the G clef, the lowest note of a viola (the C) requires no less than four

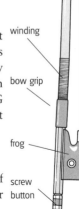

head —

stick —

bow hair —

winding

bow grip

frog

screw

button

ledger lines. This would make these low notes very hard to read. That's why viola music is written in a different clef: the *C clef*. Both the C clef and the F clef are shown on page 4.

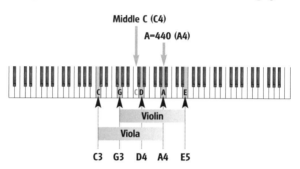

A4

The A-string of a violin sounds the same pitch as the A to the right of the Middle C on a piano keyboard. This A is known as A4 (or a', in some countries). This is also the pitch to which most musicians tune their instruments. The pitches of the other strings are indicated in the illustration.

CHILDREN'S INSTRUMENTS

A full-size violin is too big for most children under twelve. That's why there are violins in small or *fractional* sizes. Violas come in fractional sizes too.

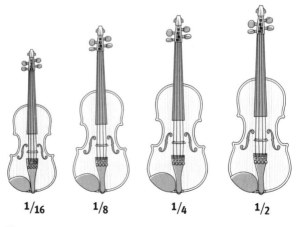

Violin and viola sizes

An 'adult' violin is usually referred to as a *full-size violin*. On paper this is shown as ⁴⁄₄. A ¹⁄₁₆ violin is actually about half as big. The illustration below shows most of the common sizes.

Viola sizes are expressed in inches, referring to the length of the body of the instrument. Adults typically play a 16" or 16.5" viola. A 12" viola is about as big as a ½ violin.

A half or a quarter

There is no absolute rule for which size goes with which age. One seven-year-old might be better off with a ¼ violin, while another child of that age needs a half-size. That's why you always need to try the instrument for size, and the same goes for the bow. A teacher will know how, and so will a good salesperson or a violin maker. Not only the child's finger and arm lengths count, but also factors like the strength of their fingers.

String length

Violins also differ in *string length* or *scale*, which is the distance from the nut to the bridge. For example, a ½ violin with a relatively large string length may be the right choice for a 'half-size' violinist with fairly big hands. More about string length is on pages 29–30 and 126.

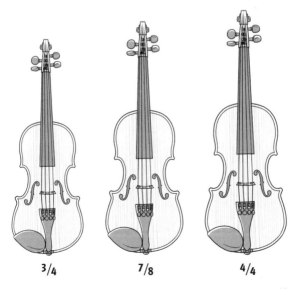

3/4   **7/8**   **4/4**

3. LEARNING TO PLAY

The violin may not be the easiest instrument to get started on, but it won't take years before you can perform on it. A chapter about learning to play, lessons, and practicing.

When you just start out, you need to get used to the feeling of having an instrument between your chin and your shoulder. Also, your left hand may initially feel like it's bent at an odd angle—and bowing the strings isn't easy either, at first.

Pizzicato   **Tipcode VIOLIN-004**

You can also play the violin by plucking the strings with your fingers. This is known as *pizzicato*. Many teachers start their pupils off with this technique to get them accustomed to using the left hand.

No markers

To play the violin in tune, you have to put your fingers in exactly the right places on the fingerboard. This too takes time to learn, as a violin's fingerboard has no markers or frets, like a guitar.

Finding the exact place...

Techniques

Of course, teachers have developed various techniques to make learning the violin less hard than it may sound here—and there are thousands of young violinists to demonstrate that it can be done.

LESSONS

If you take violin lessons, you'll learn about everything connected with playing the instrument—from bowing technique and reading music to a good posture.

Locating a teacher

Are your looking for a private teacher? Violin makers may be able to refer you to a teacher, and music stores may have teachers on staff. You can also consult your local Musicians' Union, or the orchestra teacher at a high school in your vicinity. You may also check the classified ads in newspapers, in music magazines, or on supermarket bulletin boards, or consult the *Yellow Pages*.

Professional private teachers will usually charge between twenty and fifty dollars per hour. Some make house calls, for which you'll pay extra.

Group or individual lessons

Instead of taking individual lessons, you can also go for group lessons if that's an option in your vicinity. Private lessons are more expensive, but can be tailored exactly to your needs.

Collectives

You also may want to check whether there are any teacher collectives or music schools in your vicinity. These collectives may offer extras such as ensemble playing, master classes, and clinics, in a wide variety of styles, and at various levels.

Questions, questions

On your first visit to a teacher, don't simply ask how much it costs. Here are some other questions.

• Is an introductory lesson included? This is a good way to find out how well you get on with the teacher, and, for that matter, with the instrument.

- Is the teacher interested in taking you on as a student if you are just doing it for the fun of it, or are you expected to practice at least three hours a day?
- Do you have to make a large investment in method books right away, or is course material provided?
- Can you record your lessons, so that you can listen at home to how you sound, and once more to what's been said?
- Is this teacher going to make you practice scales for two years, or will you be pushed onto a stage as soon as possible?

Not classical
Because violinists mainly play classical music, many violin teachers give 'classical' lessons. Of course, some teachers are equally at home in other musical styles, if not more so. That said, you can always benefit from what 'classical' teachers have to offer too, regardless of your own style.

PRACTICE
You can play without learning to read music—even the violin—and you can learn to play without a teacher. But there's no substitute for practice.

Three times ten
How long should you practice? That depends on your talent and on what you want to achieve. As an indication: Half an hour a day usually results in steady progress. If playing half an hour at a stretch seems too long, try dividing it up into two quarter-hour sessions, or three of ten minutes each.

A practice mute
Tipcode VIOLIN-005

Violins don't make a lot of noise, but they are loud enough to bother other people when you are practicing. There are various ways to overcome this. First of all, you can buy a *practice mute*, available in wood, metal, and rubber, for some five to fifteen dollars. You simply slide this short, thick 'comb' onto the bridge of your violin, where it effectively mutes most of the sound you produce—so it's best not to use one if your working on your tone. Other types of mutes are covered in Chapter 8.

Tissue

If you lay a paper tissue over the body, covering the *f*-holes, the sound will become a little softer still. What's more, the rosin which comes off the bow when you play won't land on your violin, which saves on cleaning. You can use the practice mute to fix the tissue to the bridge.

Electric violin

Another, more expensive solution would be to buy an electric violin. Some of these instruments have been specifically designed for silent practicing. You play them using a pair of headphones; the extremely modest sound of the strings is amplified by a small built-in amp. There's more on electric violins in Chapter 9.

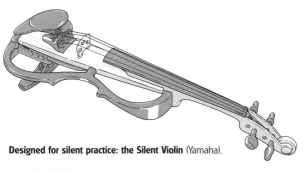

Designed for silent practice: the Silent Violin (Yamaha).

Practice violin

Practice violins or *mute violins* have become rare: They're violins without a soundbox, basically, so nobody hears you playing—but you don't hear yourself either. This makes it unsuitable for working on your intonation or timbre, for instance.

On CD

Most violin music is played together with other string instruments, with a piano, or with a complete orchestra. There's an easy way to get hold of those other musicians: buy a CD or CD-ROM. For instance, you can get special practice CDs with the same piece of music recorded three times: The first time very slowly with piano and violin, so that you can play along with the violin. The next time faster with just the piano. Then once more with a full orchestra, in the tempo in which the piece is supposed to be played. These CDs usually come with sheet music.

Lessons on your computer

There are also CD-ROMs you can play along to. Of course, you will need to have a computer handy. Some CD-ROMs even let you decide how fast a piece should be played or whether you want to hear the violin part or not.

Metronome

Most pieces of music are supposed to be played in the same tempo from beginning to end. Playing with a metronome now and then helps you to learn how to play at a constant tempo. A metronome is a small mechanical or electronic device that ticks or bleeps out a steady adjustable pulse, so you can tell immediately if you're dragging or speeding.

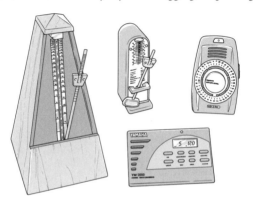

Two mechanical and two electronic metronomes.

Recording

If you record your lessons, you can listen to what was said, and especially how you sounded, when you get home. Hearing yourself play is very helpful. That's why many musicians record themselves. All you need is a portable recorder with a built-in microphone—although better equipment yields better and more enjoyable results.

Listen and play

Finally, visit festivals, concerts, and other performances. Go watch and listen to orchestras, string quartets, and other ensembles. One of the best ways to learn to play is seeing other musicians at work. Living legends or local amateurs—every concert's a learning experience. And the best way to learn to play? Play a lot!

4. BUYING OR RENTING?

What does a violin cost? Somewhere between a few hundred and a few million dollars... A guide to violin prices, and to buying or renting an instrument.

Children under twelve often start off on a rented instrument, which can be easily exchanged for a larger size after you've grown a bit. Even if you are well beyond that age, renting a violin or viola can be a good way to start, to find out either if you like playing the instrument at all, or if you like a specific instrument.

Rental fees

You can rent a full-sized student violin from around fifteen dollars a month, complete with bow and case. Insurance may be included. If not, insurance rates vary from a just a couple to ten dollars or more per month. Fractional-sized instruments are not always cheaper to rent.

Rent-to-own

Some companies offer a rent-to-own program: If you choose to buy an instrument later on, the rental fee, or part of it, will be applied against the retail price. There's a wide and pretty confusing variety of rental and rent-to-own programs, so always read the agreement carefully before you sign it, and compare what various violin dealers or music stores are offering.

Try before you buy

It's also possible to rent a more expensive instrument, so you can take your time to assess its quality. For example, you may rent a forty thousand dollar instrument for six hundred dollars per month, the rental fee equaling 1.5% of the list price.

BUYING A VIOLIN?

If you're looking for a decent, good-sounding violin that you can enjoy playing for a good few years, many dealers and teachers will tell you to spend some eight to twelve hundred dollars or more, and add at least another two or three hundred for a basic bow and a case.

Cheaper instruments

Of course there are plenty of people who have had years of fun playing a much cheaper instrument. After all, you can buy a complete *outfit* (violin, bow, and case) for as little as three or four hundred dollars, or even less. That said, there are cheap violins that are barely playable unless you have a lot of work done to them—even if they are labeled 'shop adjusted.'

Shop adjustment

Basically, every production violin needs an additional shop adjustment before it can be played. This adjustment, also known as setting up the instrument, would include making sure that the bridge, nut, sound post, fingerboard, and tuning pegs perfectly fit the instrument, and other jobs to make it perfectly playable.

Better, finer, richer

If you buy a more expensive violin, the higher price probably means that more time and attention has been devoted to its manufacture, that better wood has been used and that all the components are better matched to each other. Altogether that goes to make a better-looking, richer-sounding instrument, which may well be easier— and more fun—to play.

Better but cheaper

That said, you may very well find a new six hundred dollar instrument which performs and looks better than a new one priced at a thousand dollars, depending, for one thing, on where the instrument was made.

A good sound for less

The most important tip when you go to buy your first instrument is to take someone along who knows something about it. They will be able to tell you if a violin sounds much better than its price suggests, or the other way around. If you don't know a violinist you can take with you, try asking your teacher. And if you can't find anyone at all, at least buy one from someone who plays the instrument.

STUDENT AND MASTER VIOLINS?

All kinds of names are used to classify violins: from student violins to orchestra violins, workshop violins, and master violins. What's what, and what do these names mean?

To begin with...

Sometimes you find violins classified as student violins, orchestra violins, and concert violins. These names suggest that you should start off with the first, buy an orchestra violin once you are good enough to play in an orchestra, and move on to a concert violin as soon as you're ready to play a solo concert… Similarly, there are conservatory and artist violins.

Problem

The problem with these names is that everyone has their own ideas about what they mean. For instance, some master violin makers build 'student violins' that sell for ten times the price of a mass-produced 'concert violin'. So don't pay any attention to the names. The price of an instrument will usually tell you more.

Handmade

'Handmade' is another word that can be misleading. Plenty of low-cost production violins have largely or entirely been built by hand—but that doesn't necessarily mean they're good instruments.

Master violins

The term 'master violin' can be just as vague. Officially, though, master violins are made from start to finish by a master violin maker. They usually cost some ten thousand dollars or more, and you'd have to be prepared to join a year-long waiting list for delivery. It goes without saying that a master violin maker or *luthier* does everything by hand—so there's no need to use the word 'handmade'.

Workshop violins

The term workshop violins usually refers to instruments that others may call intermediate or step-up violins, in the price range of about a thousand dollars and more. These are often good, handmade instruments, but they're produced in series, rather than by one master luthier.

Old production instruments

Older factory-made violins can fetch a relatively high price, because many violinists believe that old instruments sound better, or more 'genuine.' Even so, a brand new violin costing eight hundred dollars may well be a better instrument than a twelve-hundred-dollar violin that was built in the early 1900s, for example.

Has to be good

On the other hand, an old and well-maintained factory-made violin that has been played a lot almost *has* to be a good violin. After all, nobody would play a violin much that doesn't sound good or isn't enjoyable to play.

Violas and small violins

Violas are more expensive than violins of the same quality. That's because they are bigger, but mainly because fewer of them are made. The same goes for bows, strings, and cases. Similarly, fractional-sized violins are not always that much cheaper than full-sized instruments.

True story

A true story. A violinist goes to buy an expensive violin. He plays, looks, and listens, plays and listens some more, and then he makes his choice: This violin is the one for him. He's absolutely sure of it. But he doesn't buy it because, to his shock and surprise, he is told that he picked the cheapest instrument available, priced at only ten thousand dollars—and he was actually looking for a instrument of at least five times that price. It really happened, and not just once…

BUYING TIPS

The main buying tip? Always buy your instrument from people who understand—and love—violins, as they won't send you home with a barely playable instrument, and they will be able to guide you in the sometimes confusing world of the violin, with its numerous brand names and countries of origin. Chapter 15 tells you more about this.

Where to buy?

You can buy violins in general music stores, which often sell mainly lower-priced production instruments, and also at specialized violin dealers and violin makers. Besides expensive handmade (master) violins, many violin makers sell cheaper instruments too.

On approval

In some cases you may be able to take an instrument on approval, so that you can assess it at home at your leisure. This is more common with expensive instruments than cheap ones, and you are more likely to be given the option if you are a good violinist than if you are choosing your first instrument.

Label

You can buy a good violin on eBay, through a classified ad or at an auction, if you know what to look for. A word of warning, though: There are thousands of violins around with labels bearing the name Stradivarius, or the name of another famous violin maker. Anyone can make labels. Making violins is harder.

Antonio Stradivarius Cremonenfis
Faciebat Anno 1999

Just about anyone can make a label...

Appraisal

If you find a secondhand instrument anywhere else than at a reputable violin dealer or maker, it's best to have it appraised before you buy. Violin makers can usually tell you exactly what a violin should cost. They'll also tell you anything that's wrong with it, and what it will cost to put it right. An appraisal may cost one or more percent of the value of the violin. If that doesn't amount to much, you may have to pay a minimum charge instead.

Buying online
You can also buy musical instruments online or by mail-order. This makes it impossible to compare instruments. Online and mail-order companies usually offer a return service for most or all of their products: If you're not happy with your purchase, you can send it back within a certain period of time. Of course the instrument should be in new condition when you send it back.

Time
Take your time when you go to buy an instrument. After all, you want it to last you for a long time. Only if you fall in love with a violin or viola should you buy it straight away. Or perhaps a week later, or once you can afford it…

Fairs and conventions
One last tip: If a violin or viola convention is being held in your vicinity, try to attend it. Besides lots of instruments you can try out and compare, you will also come across plenty of product specialists, as well as numerous fellow violinists and violists who are always a good source of information and inspiration.

MORE AND MORE EXPENSIVE
Professional violinists and conservatory students often play instruments worth tens of thousands of dollars, and there are even violins that cost more than a million. How do they get so expensive, and who can afford them?

Like paintings
Violins by famous makers like Stradivarius, Amati or Guarnerius don't cost so much only because they're so good, but also because they are at least three hundred years old: They're rare, just like the famous great paintings from that era.

Better?
Age doesn't make violins better as much as it does make

them more expensive. You can easily pay four times as much—or more—for a high-quality old instrument as for an equally good new violin.

Less famous, less expensive
The price of an old violin also depends on how well-known the maker is. You can buy a very good, rare German violin which is the same age as a Stradivarius for less than ten thousand dollars.

Reasonable?
When discussing old and expensive violins, you need to be careful with words like good, bad or reasonable. For every expert who claims that you can get a 'reasonable violin' for some three to five thousand dollars, there's another expert who will tell you that 'reasonable' starts at no less than thirty to fifty thousand dollars.

A few years or fifteen minutes
Come to that, some experts say that a new violin will start sounding really good after a few years of playing, while others say it takes fifteen minutes at most...

Conservatory students
Some conservatory students rent their expensive instruments, others are able to buy, and still others complete their education with a decent violin that costs just a few thousand dollars. Also, there are foundations that lend expensive instruments to talented students and professional musicians.

5. A GOOD VIOLIN

When you first start playing, all violins seem to look and sound the same. This chapter shows you the differences between them and tells you how to audition them, covering varnishes and wood, sizes, tops and arches, bridges, necks, pegs—and sound, of course.

How a violin sounds depends a lot on how it was built and on the quality of the wood. But the strings are important too, and so is the bow, and the adjustment of the instrument. These three subjects are dealt with in Chapters 6, 7, and 11.

Purely by ear

The first and major part of this chapter is about everything there is to see on violins and violas, and what it all means for how they sound. If you prefer to choose an instrument using your ears only, then you can skip ahead to the tips on pages 42–45.

The looks

Violins come in glossy and matte finishes, and some instruments have a warm, satin-like glaze. When it comes to their color, there are even more variations. Some are pale orange or even yellowish, others have a rich amber or a deep brown hue, and still others tend toward red or purple. Violins in completely different colors, such as green or blue, are rare.

Oil and spirit

Traditionally, violins have an oil-based finish, which used

to take weeks to dry. Today, these finishes can be dried using ultraviolet light, and you may be able to find oil-varnished violins for as little as three or four hundred dollars. Spirit-based varnishes are used on violins in most price ranges. Be aware that spirit- and oil-based finishes on inexpensive instruments tend to be quite brittle.

Invisible repairs

No one finish is typically better than any other. What's really important is that repairs and scratches can be touched up invisibly with both oil-based and spirit-based varnishes. Nitrocellulose lacquer, when applied properly, is another type of finish that allows for invisible repairs.

Synthetic varnishes

Low-priced violins can have a synthetic finish (*i.e.,* polyurethane) too. This glossy type of finish can be applied very quickly, using spray guns, and it's strong, hard, and easy to clean. Being so hard, on the other hand, it may reduce the instrument's sound potential, especially if it has been applied very thickly. Another drawback is that it doesn't allow for invisible repairs.

Shading

Violins are not always the same color all over. Older violins sometimes have lighter patches where they have been handled a great deal. These worn-out patches are sometimes imitated on new violins too. This technique, *shading*, makes a violin look older than it really is.

Checked finish

Older violins often have a *checked finish*, the varnish being marked with a fine web of tiny cracks. This effect, also known as *craquelure*, can be imitated by the maker too. Yet another way to make an instrument look older is to bring out the grain by applying a dark dye.

Aged to order

Antiquing is a generic name for making a violin look older than it is, which often raises its price. If you have an instrument custom-built, you can of course ask the violin maker to 'antique' it for you. Even minor damage, small repairs, and worn-out spots can be imitated.

Flamed wood

The wood of the backs and ribs of many violins looks like it's been licked by flames. This *flamed*, *figured* or *curled wood* is common on more expensive violins, but you may find it in the lowest price range also. Whether the wood is

plain, or slightly, medium, or well flamed does not relate to its quality or sound potential. On the other hand, beautifully flamed wood has its price. In student and intermediate price ranges the highly flamed instruments are often the most expensive ones.

Bookmatched

Many flamed backs clearly show that they're made up of two very precisely mirrored or *bookmatched* halves (see pages 114–115).

A mirrored, flamed back.

Fine or clumsy

Most scrolls look like a perfect spiral, with sharply carved, smooth edges. Others look more clumsily carved. Are these violins no good? No: Clumsy scrolls may even be rarer on mass-produced instruments than on hand-carved violins.

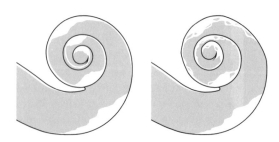

A perfect spiral, or a clumsy job...

Slightly different

Every scroll is slightly different, from maker to maker and from brand to brand. The more you look, the more differences you will see. One example would be the *fluting*, *i.e.*, the carved grooves in the back of the scroll.

Purfling

The inlaid purfling, usually consisting of three strips of wood, is not just for decoration. It also protects the instrument, preventing cracks at the edge from extending to the *plates* (top and back). Double purfling is rare, but you may come across it. A tip: On cheap violins, the purfling is sometimes not inlaid, but painted onto the wood.

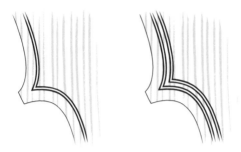

Purfling usually consists of three or more inlaid strips of wood.

THE BODY

The body of one violin may be a little higher or wider than another, or a little slimmer at the waist, or the top may be slightly more or less arched. And violas come in different sizes. A tour of the body.

(Not) all the same

Full-size violins are all pretty much the same size, to the nearest fraction of an inch. Full-size violas, however, come in sizes from 15" to 17" (body length) in half-inch increments. Most adult violists use a 16" or 16.5" viola.

Larger

There are beautiful small violas around, but usually a larger model will sound both 'larger' and fuller—which is what most violists prefer. If you like or need a smaller one, you may want to look for an instrument that's a little wider and deeper. This would make it more likely to sound like a 'real' viola than a short model that's also narrow and shallow.

Stop

Especially on large violas you may find yourself sounding *flat* (too low) in certain positions. This may be due to the fact that the instrument has a deviant *stop*, *f-stop*, or *mensur ratio*. These technical terms refer to the relationship between the distances from the nut to the top edge of the body, and from the top edge to the notches in the *f*-holes (see *String length*, page 128).

Slimmer waist

Being able to see the subtle differences between one violin and the next takes time, patience, and a lot of practice. Some instruments have noticeably wider bodies than others, or just a wider or a slimmer waist (the *C-bout*) This hardly affects the sound, but it can mean that one violin fits you better than another, especially in how easy it is to reach the highest positions on the fingerboard.

Stradivarius

Many violins are still based on the instrument that Stradivarius designed around 1700. The names of other violin makers are used to indicate other models. Again, the differences are small, but they're well documented. A Stradivarius model is a little wider and has shorter *f*-holes than a Guarnerius model, for example.

The top

The top is the most important part of a violin: When you play, the strings make the top vibrate, and it is mainly these vibrations that determine the sound of your violin. The top is the *soundboard* of the instrument.

Spruce

The top, also known as *table* or *belly*, is almost always made of a solid piece of spruce, which has been carved into shape. Spruce is also used for the bass bar and the sound post.

Maple

The back is usually made of one or two pieces of solid maple, a slightly heavier and denser wood. Cheap violins may have a laminated back, made up of several plies. Maple is used for the ribs and the neck as well.

Fine grain

Violinists often prefer the top to have a grain that is straight, even, and not too wide, getting gradually finer toward the center of the instrument. Of course, some violins have a beautiful grain but don't sound good, and there are great violins with an uneven, wide grain as well.

The arching

A top with a lower arching will often help produce a stronger, more powerful sound than one with a high arching. Most violin tops are between 0.6" and 0.7" (15–18 mm) high. The back is usually a little flatter.

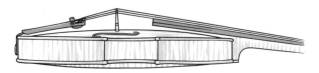

The back is a little flatter than the top.

The channel

A violin with a deep, broad channel will often have a softer sound than an instrument that barely has this 'valley' along the edge.

Flowing lines

You can spend hours looking at violin archings. They all look similar, yet they are all slightly different. What is especially important is that the lines of the arch flow, that there are no flat parts or odd angles, and that the arching isn't too high, too low, or too narrow. The more often you look, the more you'll see.

Thick and thin

Low-cost violins and violas often have thick tops, which are easier to make. A top that is too thick will make for a thin sounding instrument. Master violin makers measure the thickness of a top to hundredths of an inch, making the instrument produce the sound they have in mind.

Graduated top and back

Good instruments have a *graduated* top and back, the exact thickness of the plates varying from spot to spot.

The ribs

In a full-sized violin, the ribs are usually little more than an inch high all the way around. A relatively shallow instrument may sound thin, and a violin that is too deep may have a hollow sound. Violas are often deeper by the tailpiece than they are at the neck end.

Hot hide glue

Violin makers use hot hide (animal) glue for their instruments. Joints—or *seams*—fixed with this type of glue can be loosened again if necessary. This allows a violin maker or technician to take the top off for repairs. Cheap production violins may use types of glue that prevent such repairs.

NECK AND FINGERBOARD

The neck and fingerboard affect both the playability and sound of a violin. They can also tell you something about how well-made the instrument is.

Ebony

Fingerboards are almost always made of ebony. This is a nearly black, extremely hard type of wood. The smoother and more even the fingerboard, the more easily it plays. Cheap violins sometimes have fingerboards of softer, light-colored wood, which is often painted black to make it look like ebony. You can sometimes recognize them by lighter patches or blank spots on the sides. After years of use, even the hardest fingerboard will wear, after which it should be reworked or, eventually, replaced (see Chapter 11, *Violin Maintenance*).

Thick fingers

The grooves in the nut, at the top of the fingerboard, determine the string spacing and the string height at that end. Nuts can be replaced to adjust both string spacing

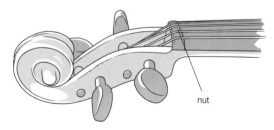

nut

The nut can be replaced.

and height. For example, if you have thick fingers, you may prefer a nut with grooves set a little further apart.

Feel the neck

Necks are always much lighter in color; a dark neck would soon show worn patches. On more expensive violins, the wood is usually not varnished but protected with a little oil. Feel if the curve of the neck lies nicely in your hand and that there are no odd pits or bumps. Note that necks come in different thicknesses.

Concave fingerboard

The fingerboard is very slightly concave along its length. This prevents the stings from buzzing when playing in the higher positions.

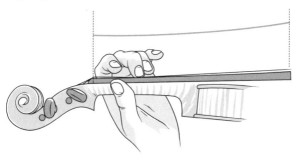

The fingerboard: slightly curved.

Straight

If you look at the neck and fingerboard lengthwise, they should of course be straight, set exactly in the center line of the violin, and not look as though someone has tried to wrench the instrument out of shape.

In between the notches

If you hold the violin with the tailpiece toward you, you can check whether the bridge is exactly between the two notches of the f-holes. If so, then check that the strings run perfectly straight along the fingerboard.

Downwards

If you look from the side, you'll see that the neck is tilted slightly downwards. Before 1800, this was not the case. In those days, there was a 90-degree angle between the neck and the side of the body. This made these instruments produce less volume: The large neck angle reduces the pressure of the strings on the bridge. Conversely, a smaller neck angle means more pressure on the bridge, which makes the sound bigger, louder, or more radiant.

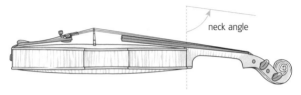

neck angle

A smaller neck angle gives a bigger sound.

Baroque violins

To play Baroque music, violinists often prefer to use a special Baroque violin. The mellow sound of these violins is due to a larger neck angle and other factors, including the use of gut strings (unwound, except for the G) and a different string length. Baroque violins are played without a chin rest.

STRING HEIGHT

The string height is the distance between the strings and the fingerboard. Having your strings very high above the fingerboard makes it hard work to play. If they are too low, they may buzz against the fingerboard. In between, it's largely a matter of taste and the type of strings you're using. A greater string height (also referred to as a *higher action*) can give your instrument a slightly clearer, brighter or more powerful sound.

Room to move

At the nut, the snares are very close to the fingerboard. At the other end of the fingerboard, the distance between the fingerboard and the strings is a lot bigger. There, the thick strings are always slightly higher above the fingerboard than the thin ones, because they need more room to move.

The figures

On a violin, the E-string usually is some 0.12" (3 mm) above the fingerboard, while the G-string will be at about

0.16" to 0.20" (4–5 mm). Gut strings need a greater string height, and steel strings need to be a little closer to the fingerboard. Add 0.02" (0.5 mm) to each of these measurements for violas.

Too high

If you have a new violin that has not yet been properly adjusted, the strings will probably be too high. Adjusting may involve replacing or lowering the bridge and the nut.

THE BRIDGE

The bridge matters not only for the string height, but also for the sound of the instrument.

Straight

Bridges are a bit slanted at the front and straight at the back. The straight back must be perpendicular to the violin's top, and the bridge's feet should be exactly between the notches of the *f*-holes.

Flecked

Some bridges are plain, while others may be highly flecked or speckled, the latter called *Spiegelholz* in German. In itself, this difference tells you nothing about the quality of the wood: Non-flecked, slightly flecked, and highly flecked wood is used for

A flecked bridge: cheap or expensive...

both cheap and expensive bridges. A fine, straight grain is more important.

(Un)treated

Violin catalogs often indicate whether bridges are treated or untreated, which refers to the bridges being finished with varnish or oil. Some feel that this treatment enhances the quality of the bridge; other experts prefer to use untreated ones.

Bridges and sound

Of course you're not going to weigh a bridge when you're choosing a violin, but it's worth knowing that a heavy bridge can muffle the sound slightly, just like a mute (see page 74). A very light bridge may be the culprit if an instrument has a very thin, weak, or uncentered tone. The hardness of the wood also plays a role. A bridge made of harder wood helps produce more volume and a stronger, brighter tone.

Models

Bridges come in different models, but you'll need to look very carefully to tell them apart. Violin makers and technicians do see those differences, and they know which bridge is best for your instrument.

Blanks

The bridges you find in stores and catalogs are blanks: Bridges always need to be custom-fit to your instrument.

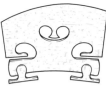

There are bridges with moveable feet that automatically adjust to the arch of the top—but even if you prefer this type of bridge, it can't hurt to have a specialist install it: Properly fitting a bridge to an instrument involves more than carving the feet (see also page 102).

An adjustable bridge with moveable feet.

Not too deep

The longer an instrument has been played, the further the strings will wear into the bridge. If the grooves have become too deep, the strings will be muffled, and harder to tune. The string height will be decreased as well, and the strings may break sooner. Ideally, the grooves should be just so deep that two-thirds of the thickness of each string sticks out above the bridge.

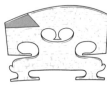

Cutting string

The E-string, no more than 0.01" (0.25 mm) thick, is the one most likely to cut into your bridge. That's why some bridges have a piece of bone or hardwood set into them at this point. A plastic sleeve

A bridge with an ebony inset.

(see page 55) or a piece of vellum (parchment; see page 100) will also help.

Two at once

The top of the bridge has almost the same curve as the top of the fingerboard: It is highest in the middle and lowest by the thinnest string. Beginners often prefer a highly-curved bridge: The higher curve reduces the chance of inadvertently bowing two strings instead of one. Conversely, if you want to play two or even three strings simultaneously, you will need a bridge with a lower curve.

Collapsed bridges

Nearly all bridges collapse slightly in time with the pressure of the strings. A violin will produce its best sound with a straight bridge—so have your bridge replaced in time (see page 102).

High bridges

Most bridges are between 0.12" and 0.14" (31–35 mm) high at their topmost point. If a bridge is too high, the sound may become a little hollow (and the action may be too high!). Sometimes a high bridge is used to compensate for a very small neck angle.

THE SOUND POST

Inside the body, slightly behind the bridge, is the sound post. This thin round spruce stick is not just there for strength: It also has a lot to do with the sound. French violin makers even call it *l'âme*: the soul of the violin.

Fractions

The sound post must be straight, and long enough to be firmly wedged but not so long that it pushes the top and the back apart. The exact position is critical too, measured to less than a twentieth of an inch (1 mm).

Adjustment

A violin maker can adjust the sound of a violin by moving the sound post a fraction. This way a violin can be made slightly less edgy, or a little clearer, for example. Also, if one string sounds louder or softer than the others, having the sound post repositioned may be the solution. Alternatively, you may try using different strings—but that's another chapter (Chapter 6, to be precise).

PEGS AND FINE TUNERS

You can tune a violin with the wooden tuning pegs at the top. Depending on the strings you use, for one thing, you'll use the fine tuners in the tailpiece as well, or instead. Both pegs and fine tuners come in different types and sizes.

Hardwood

Pegs get thicker toward the thumb piece. This tapered shape prevents them from twisting loose by themselves. They are usually made of ebony, which is also used for tailpieces and chin rests. Rosewood and boxwood are popular too. Rosewood has a reddish-brown color; boxwood is usually yellowish. A violin with a full-ebony trim has ebony parts all over.

Breaking strings

Very cheap violins sometimes have pegs made out of a softer type of wood, into which the strings may soon wear grooves. When a string jams in a groove, it is very likely to break soon.

A good fit

Cheap violins are often hard to tune, or they go out of tune quickly because the pegs are of poor quality or don't fit properly. Tuning pegs should turn easily, but not slip.

Parisian eyes

Pegs come with various peg head designs, a familiar one being an inverted heart with a ball on top. Another type of

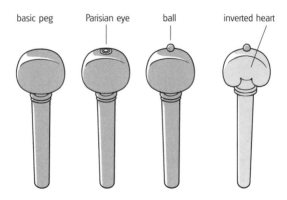

basic peg   Parisian eye   ball   inverted heart

Tuning pegs.

decoration is a *Parisian eye:* a small, mother-of-pearl dot with a metal ring around it. A single mother-of-pearl dot is simply called an (*single*) *eye* or an *eyelet.*

Fine tuners
Tipcode VIOLIN-006

Certain types of strings (*e.g.,* steel strings) can best be tuned with *fine tuners.* Less expensive violins usually have four fine tuners built into the tailpiece, but you can also buy them separately. Many violinists combine three gut strings with a single steel string (high E), which will then be the only string to have a fine tuner.

Fine tuners and synthetic strings

Fine tuners can be used for some types of synthetic strings as well, but not with all of them: The strings may be too thick to fit the fine tuner, or the fine tuner may cause string breakage.

Names and lengths

Fine tuners come with many different names (*adjusters, tuning adjusters, string tuners, string adjusters…*) and in different shapes and sizes. Longer models stick out a little from below the tailpiece. If you use short ones, you won't see much of them besides the thumb screws. Some well-known models of short fine tuners include Hill, Uni, and Piccolo.

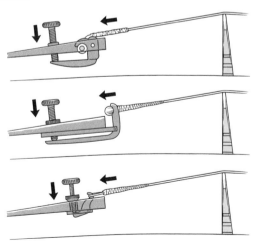

A built-in fine tuner (above), long and short fine tuners.

Easier

Long fine tuners make tuning a little easier than short ones, because you need less power to operate them. Fitting new strings becomes easier too. If the tailpiece of the violin is very close to the top, perhaps because the top has a high arch, you can be better off with short ones: Long fine tuners may damage the top when turned too far. Some models are provided with cushions to prevent this.

Short or long

There are violinists who prefer to have short fine tuners because long ones reduce the length of the string between bridge and tailpiece, which they consider bad for the sound. There are at least as many good violinists who say you'll never hear the difference.

Loop or ball

Most strings have a ball at the end that fits the fine tuner. Steel E-strings come with either a ball or a loop. Ball-end strings require a fine tuner with two prongs, while loop-end strings can be attached to both one and two-prong fine tuners. There are also special fine tuners for gut strings, and versions with an extra wide slot for heavy-gauge strings: Using a thick string in a narrow slot may result in string breakage. Most fine tuners cost between two and five dollars each.

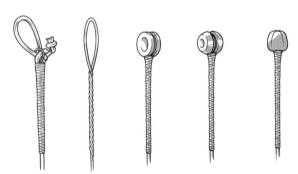

Some strings have a loop, others a ball end.

Geared pegs

Rather than using fine tuners, you may have a modern type of tuning mechanism installed, which incorporates a built-in gear system. These *geared pegs* or *planetary pegs* allow for much finer tuning than a conventional wood peg, they don't stick or slip, and they are maintenance-free.

TAILPIECE

Tailpieces, believe it or not, may also influence the sound of your instrument. They come in various materials and designs, and with or without decoration or built-in fine tuners.

Slim or angular

There is a great variety of tailpieces available, especially in wood. Two examples of well-known basic designs would be the French model, with a very slim upper part, or the Hill model, named after a British manufacturer, with elegant lines and an angular end.

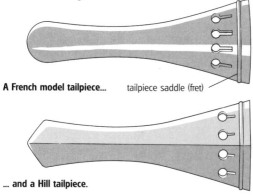

A French model tailpiece...   tailpiece saddle (fret)

... and a Hill tailpiece.

Parallel

The strings should always run parallel between the bridge and the tailpiece. If not, the tailpiece is too narrow or too wide for the instrument.

Golden saddle

If you have gold-colored fine tuners, you might like the *tailpiece saddle* or *fret* to be in the same color. Usually, this little ridge is black. You can also get other decorations on tailpieces, such as a Parisian eye or an inlaid figure.

The sound

The tailpiece has roughly the same effect on the sound of the violin as the bridge. A heavy tailpiece can slightly muffle the sound, making it a little less bright, somewhat similar to what a heavy bridge or a light mute would do. Conversely, a lighter tailpiece gives a clearer, brighter sound. The sound may becomes a bit uncentered too— just like with a bridge that is too light.

All together

Of course, these differences are not that obvious—but if you use a heavy tailpiece that is too close to the bridge (see page 103) and has four big, long fine tuners in it, the extra mass near the bridge can make your instrument sound noticeably duller.

Viola tailpieces

Because violas come in different lengths, viola tailpieces do too. It's important to have one that is the right length for your instrument, as this length determines the important string length from the bridge to the tailpiece (again, see page 103). Viola tailpieces often have the size of the viola they are made for marked on the bottom.

PLAY-TESTING TIPS

If you try ten violins in a row, you'll have forgotten what the first one sounded like by the time you try the last. The play-testing tips given below make it easier to compare violins.

Take it with you

If you already have a violin, take it with you when you go to choose another instrument. Comparing it with a different violin makes it easier to judge what you hear. If you have your own bow, take that with you too. Otherwise, use the best bow available in the store. Using a good bow will give you a better idea of what the different violins are capable of.

Someone else

If you don't play yourself, or have only just started, you won't know whether an instrument has a poor sound, or whether it's just you. So ask someone who does play to demonstrate the different violins to you. That someone could also be the violin maker, for instance.

By ear

If you ask someone else to play, you can also hear how the violin sounds from a distance. The sound will be quite different compared to having it right by your ear. Another tip: If you simply can't choose between a few violins or violas, turn around. Then you won't know which instrument is being played, so you'll really be choosing only by ear. You won't see the price tag, the finish, the brand name, or the age anymore. Sometimes musicians choose much cheaper instruments than they expected to by ear—but it may be the other way around too.

Very different

A tip: Start by listening to two very different violins, one with a bright sound, and one with a mellow, dark sound. Knowing these extremes may make your search easier.

Three

First, make a rough selection of the instruments you like on first hearing. Take three of them, and compare them with one another. Replace the one you like least by another violin from your rough selection. Compare the three again—and so on.

Play something simple

If you have a lot of violins to choose from, it's often easier if you only play briefly on each one. Play something simple, so that you can concentrate on the instrument, rather than on what you play. Even a scale will do. When you have a few violins left, and you really need to choose, you'll probably want to play longer and more demanding pieces so that you can get to know the instruments better.

String by string

You can also compare violins string by string or note by note. How does the open E-string sound? Do all four strings sound equally loud, and how does the instrument sound in the highest positions? How do they sound when you pluck them, or when you play long notes?

The same

The violins that you are comparing must be tuned properly and to the same pitch. Otherwise, one violin might sound a little warmer than the others, say, just because it is tuned a bit lower. For similar reasons, you should really compare instruments fitted with the same type of strings. If not, you will be comparing strings instead of violins.

LISTENING TIPS

Of course, it's impossible to put into words how different violins sound—at least words that everyone agrees on. But the following tips will make choosing an instrument with your ears a lot easier.

Volume and projection

Some violins will always sound very soft or weak, however energetically you play them. In an orchestra with one such instrument, no one will be able to hear you. Other violins can be heard at a fair distance too, even if you play very softly. A violin like that has good *projection*.

Even

The E-string not only sounds higher than the other strings, it also sounds different. If you play an E first on the open E-string, and then play the same pitch on the A- and D-strings, you'll hear that very same pitch sound with three very different *timbres*. All the same, a violin should have an even, balanced sound: The differences from string to string should not be like going from one instrument to another.

Response

A violin should have a good response. That means it sounds good and responds immediately, even when you play very softly. If not, the instrument is hard to play; it makes you really work for each note. If a violin has a poor response, it takes a little while before the tone is really 'there.' On violas, the C-string is very critical, as it's so heavy.

Uncentered tone

Some violins sound like the tone never really gets there; it may lack foundation, producing an uncentered, weak tone. Both a slow response and an uncentered tone can also be down to the strings, to the bow, to the rosin, or—sadly—to yourself.

Dynamics and colors

A violin should be able to sound just as loud or soft as you play. If it does, it has good dynamics. If it doesn't, its performance will always be a bit shallow. The instrument should also be able to produce different timbres or 'colors'. One example: If you play a little closer to the fingerboard, the sound is supposed to become noticeably rounder than if you play near the bridge—and the instrument should sound good both ways.

Preference

Apart from that, sound is mostly a matter of personal preference. Bear in mind that when two people listen to the same instrument, they'll probably use different words to describe what they hear. What one finds harsh or edgy (in other words, unpleasant), another may describe as bright and clear (in other words, pleasant), and what's warm to one ear sounds dull to another. It all depends on what you do and do not like—and how you put that into words.

Rich = more of everything

The better an instrument is, the richer it sounds. Richer means a full, resonant tone; it means there's more of everything; and it means that you're allowed to produce a wide variety of tonal colors, mellow and vivid, subdued and bright, sad and happy, shaded or direct...

Poor

Some words associated with poorer-sounding instruments are nasal (as if the violin has a cold), hollow (like you're playing in a bathroom), thin (as if it's a miniature), or dull (as if there's a blanket over it)—and everybody has more or less the same idea of what those words mean.

USED VIOLINS

When you go to buy a used instrument, there are a few extra things you should remember.

Repairs

First of all: No matter what's broken, a decent violin can almost always be fixed. Of course, if you decide to buy an instrument that needs some work, you need to know what it's going to cost first. Some types of damage are easy to see, other kinds only an expert will spot. Come to that, you need to be an expert to judge things like how well a violin has been repaired. If in doubt, take a violin for appraisal first (see also page 23).

Major damage: cracks in the sound post and bass bar areas.

What to watch out for
Here are some things to check when buying a secondhand instrument. A complete list would soon be too long for this book.

- **Violin varnish wears.** One place to check is where your left hand touches the body. If the varnish has completely gone, you may need to do something about it.
- If the type of varnish allows for it, it is usually **touched up** after repairs (see page 27). Make sure this has been done properly.
- Check the **edges**: This is where the instruments gets knocked most often. Depending on the damage, repairing damaged edges can cost up to hundreds of dollars.
- Cracks in the top or the back always run lengthwise. Cracks by **the sound post and the bass bar** are often hard to see and even harder to repair.
- Other places to check for cracks include **the shoulder of the neck and the cheeks** (sides) of the pegbox near the pegs.
- Glue can come loose—along the edges for instance, or at the neck. Tap a violin very softly with a knuckle: this can sometimes help you discover **loose glue joints**.

- If the **tuning pegs** are pushed very far into the pegbox, sticking way out at the other end, they may need to be replaced, and the holes may need to be rebushed. This is quite expensive.
- Check the **arching of the top**. Sometimes the pressure of the strings makes the top a little flatter near the bass bar, or a little higher by the sound post.

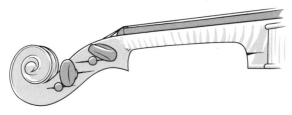

Cracks in the cheeks and the shoulder of the neck.

Woodworms

Woodworms burrow into wood and leave narrow tunnels. This can be very serious, especially if they have been at work in the top or the back. You won't find woodworms in a instrument that has always been played: This particular animal doesn't like music. If you want to know whether they're still around, lay your instrument on a piece of black cardboard overnight. If there's sawdust on the cardboard the next day, the instrument has tenants.

6. GOOD STRINGS

For hundreds of years, all violin and viola strings were made of gut. These days you can buy steel strings and synthetic-core strings as well, in many variations. Every type of string produces a different sound, some strings are easier to play than others, and some strings sound better on one violin or viola than on another.

Violin strings can last a long time—up to a year, or even longer. It does help if they are fitted properly and kept clean. More information on keeping your strings in good condition is in Chapter 11, *Violin Maintenance*.

Gut, steel, synthetic
There are three main types of strings. Originally, violins had gut strings exclusively. Then came steel strings, which sound a good deal clearer. Strings with a synthetic core didn't appear until the 1950s, but they are now the most widely used type.

Important
Strings are very important for how your violin or viola sounds and plays. The difference in sound between cheap and expensive strings can easily be much bigger than the difference between a cheaper and a (much!) more expensive instrument. The same is true for the difference between synthetic-core, steel, and gut strings.

Expensive
A tip: Try out a different set of strings once in a while, and you may want to try really expensive strings too, even on

an affordable instrument. You may be surprised by the effect they have on the sound.

Winding
Most strings are wound with ultra-thin metal ribbon. Because of this winding the string itself can be kept fairly thin, so that it responds easily, while the extra mass enables it to sound as low as it should. How a string sounds not only depends on the material of the core, but also on its winding.

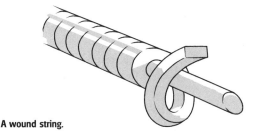

A wound string.

Hard and soft
Finally, there is also a difference between 'hard' and 'soft' strings, or strings with a higher or lower tension, and between thicker and thinner strings. This chapter tells you what you need to know about these important differences.

Prices
The prices mentioned below are for sets of four violin strings. If you buy strings separately, the thickest string will often cost two, three, or four times as much as the thinnest. Viola strings usually cost five to fifteen dollars more per set of four.

GUT STRINGS
The first violins had sheep gut strings, and there are still violinists who feel that the instrument sounds best with this type of strings. Of course gut strings are also used when playing music written in the days when these were the only strings available (*e.g.*, Baroque violins; see page 34).

Sound
The sound of gut strings is often described as mellow,

warm, and rich. They allow for great variation in color and inflection—which in turn demands a good musician. Gut strings need to be broken in: It takes a few hours of playing to get them to develop their full sound.

Tuning

As they stretch a fair bit when new, you'll have to tune gut strings quite often at first. Additional tuning is also required as gut strings detune with changes in temperature or humidity.

Expensive

Gut strings, which are used mainly by professional musicians, often don't last very long and are generally quite expensive. A set will easily cost forty to fifty dollars or more, but they're available for less as well.

Steel E

Gut E-strings are quite rare as they are very vulnerable. Even so, they are still used by some musicians, for instance those who play Baroque music (seventeenth and early eighteenth century). Most other violinists prefer to use a steel E.

Wound E or plain E

Steel E-strings are sometimes wound, but they're usually *plain strings*. A plain steel E-string usually sounds a little clearer than a wound one.

STEEL STRINGS

Steel strings offer a clear, bright, powerful sound and an immediate response. They're very reliable and they last a long time, typically from six months to a year, or even longer.

Bright

Their immediate response makes steel strings a good choice for beginners, but there's more. Because of their bright tone, steel strings sound especially good on violins which themselves have a slightly subdued sound. They're also popular with violinists who need a lot of volume and a strong, big sound.

The core

Most steel strings have a core made up of several very thin steel strands. Strings with a solid steel core help produce a stronger tone. There are also steel strings that have been specially treated to sound a little warmer.

Advantages

Steel strings have two more advantages. First, they do not have to be broken in: They sound good immediately, and they're not as stretchy as new gut or synthetic strings. Second, steel strings are not bothered by changes in temperature and humidity.

Plenty of volume

Steel sets are available for around fifteen dollars or even less, which is why most cheaper violins come with this type of strings. Professional-quality steel strings may cost up to three times as much.

The E

There are more variations on the steel E-string than on any other, with prices from one to ten or more dollars. They can be either wound or plain. (The other steel strings are always wound.) Steel E-strings can also differ in thickness and in stiffness, or the precise material used may be different.

Chrome-steel or coated steel

For example, ordinary steel easily discolors and may go out of tune as it does. You can get around this problem by using a chrome-steel string. Or you can buy an E-string with a coating of silver, gold, or another material. This ultra-thin finish protects the steel and also gives a slightly warmer sound.

SYNTHETIC STRINGS

Synthetic-core strings are the most widely used, by beginners, students, and professional string players. You could consider them 'in between' gut and steel, in terms of sound, life expectancy, and price. A set of four typically costs twenty-five to thirty-five dollars, but they come cheaper or twice as expensive as well.

Sound

As there's a large variety in synthetic-core materials and windings, there's a large variety in sound too. Generally speaking, the sound is close to that of gut strings, though a bit brighter. Compared to steel strings they sound noticeably warmer—or less hard and bright... Some of the core materials used are nylon and perlon.

Breaking them in

New synthetic-core strings may sound a bit harsh at first. If so, their sound improves after a couple of hours of playing. Also, they're a bit stretchy, so they need time to settle in. Another similarity with gut strings is that synthetic strings are often combined with a steel E-string.

WINDINGS

To make sure that the strings of a set fit together as well as possible, manufacturers often use different windings within one set of strings—silver for the G, for instance, to add a little power to this thick string, and aluminum for the next two strings, to make them sound a bit warmer.

Viola

You'll come across all kinds of combinations for violas too. Two silver and two aluminum-wound strings, perhaps, going from thick to thin. Or one silver, one chrome, and two aluminum-wound strings.

Wound steel

With steel sets, the strings will often have the same winding. Nickel or wound strings will usually make for a softer, sweeter, or warmer sound than chrome-steel windings.

More

There are many more materials used to wind strings, including copper, titanium, tungsten, and silver mixed with gold. If you are looking for a particular sound, a good salesperson or violin maker will be able to help you with your choice. But if you really want to be sure, you'll need to try out different strings for yourself. The same goes for choosing between thicker and thinner strings, or between louder and softer-sounding strings.

LOUD OR SOFT

Synthetic and steel strings often come in several varieties: *dolce* (soft), *medium*, and *forte* (strong), for instance. You may also see German descriptions like *weich* (soft) and *stark* (strong). Forte strings, also indicated as *orchestra* or *solo*, are heavier than dolce strings.

Lower tension

Softer-sounding strings have a lower tension than louder strings. Some string manufacturers describe their strings by their tension, marketing low-, medium-, and high-tension strings. Strings with a higher tension take a little more effort to play and they respond less quickly, but their brighter, stronger sound enhances the projection of your instrument. Medium strings are the most commonly used.

The instrument

Which strings are best also depends on the instrument you are playing. Using forte strings may work great on one violin, but their higher tension may actually degrade the sound on another instrument, for example.

Colors

To indicate the different types of strings, manufacturers use colored thread at one of the string's ends. At the other end, the string's pitch has been marked with another color, to prevent you from putting the D-string where the A-string should be, for example.

Confusing

Unfortunately, no uniform color codes are used, so the same color may mean one thing for one make and something else for the next.

Similarly, there's no consistency in what (string type, string pitch) is indicated at which end of the string. Confusing...

The same make and series

A tip: If the strings on a violin are of the same make and series, you will see four different colors (indicating the pitch of each string) at one end, and only one color (indicating the series or type of strings) at the other.

Mixed up

If this is not so, there's a fair chance that strings of different brands, series, or tensions have been combined in one set. If they all sound good and sound good together, that's no problem. If you want to know which strings are fitted to your instrument, ask an expert. They can usually tell from the color codes.

Thick or thin

Gut strings come in different gauges. Heavier-gauge strings are harder work to play; they may sound fuller, louder, and clearer; and they don't respond as easily as thinner strings.

How thick

If you want to know exactly how thick a gut string is in inches, divide its gauge by 500. For example, a 14 is 14÷500 = 0.028". To get millimeters, divide the gauge by 20.

String height

Fitting higher-tension strings will increase the instrument's action. Conversely, lower-tension strings will decrease the instrument's string height, as the strings reduce the tension on the neck.

Adjusting string height—by means of replacing or lowering the bridge, for example—is a job for a professional.

AND MORE

A few last tips about ball ends and loops, about how long your strings will last, and about plastic sleeves and string brands.

Ball or loop

As discussed on page 40, steel E-strings come with either a loop or a ball at the end where they attach to the fine tuner. Check your fine tuner to see which type you need.

Write it down

If you're putting new strings on your violin, you can list their details on page 133 of this book. Then you'll be able to buy the same type if you like them, or avoid them if you don't.

How long

How long your strings will last depends on many things— on how often you play, of course, but also on the core material of the strings and the type of winding, on how well you keep your strings clean, and on the type of sweat you have: If you have very acidic perspiration, you may have to take this into account when buying strings. Some windings may be able to withstand your chemical makeup better than others.

Often, experimentation is the only way to find the solution. You'll find more tips in Chapter 11, where you'll also learn how to tell when it's time to replace one or more of your strings.

Sleeves

Strings often come with little plastic sleeves around them. These prevent the strings from cutting into the bridge, and they prevent the bridge from damaging the strings. Most of the sleeve must be on the side of the tailpiece; otherwise it will muffle the sound too much.

E-string

That said, a little muffling may actually be desirable with a steel E-string, making it sound just a little sweeter. Being so thin, the same string is also the most likely one to cut into the bridge. Rubber *tone filters* are available separately, and with some strings they're included. A small piece of rubber (gasoline) tubing under the string does the same job.

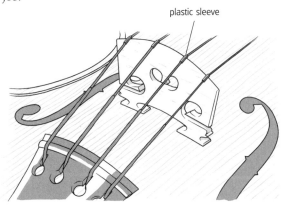

plastic sleeve

Plastic sleeves around the strings.

Fractional sizes

Fractional-sized instruments require fractional-sized strings. Regular strings will not provide the required tension, resulting in a weak tone and possible string breakage.

String brands

Choosing the right strings can also be hard because of the wide selection that is available. The three best known string makers are probably D'Addario (USA), Pirastro (Germany), and Thomastik-Infeld (Austria), each of which makes various series of strings. If you'd look just at some of their synthetic and steel strings, well-known examples would be the Pro Arte and Helicore series from D'Addario, Tonica, and Chromcor (Pirastro), and the Thomastik Dominant and Spirocore series. Examples of the many other string brands are Corelli, Jargar, John Pearse, Kaplan, Larsen, Mathias Thoma, Meisel, Pinnacle, Prim, Pyramid, Stellar, Supreme, Syntha-Core, and Super-Sensitive. Some of these companies make rosin, other accessories, or even violins too.

Custom strings

There are violinists and violists who prefer to put together their own sets of strings, combining a variety of brands, series, materials, and windings to produce a specific sound or effect, and to optimally adjust the instrument to their demands.

An octave lower

Ready for something completely different? By fitting a set of octave strings or baritone strings, you can make your violin sound an octave lower. These strings, produced by various string makers, are mostly used in experimental, avant-garde music. Your violin may need to be adapted to accept these special strings, which are considerably thicker than regular strings.

7. BOWS AND ROSINS

You'll only get the very best from your violin if you have a bow that suits both your instrument, your style of playing, and the music you play. A chapter about brazilwood and pernambuco, synthetic bows, frogs, ferrules, horsehair or synthetic hair, weight and balance, and rosin.

The stick of the bow can be made of wood or a synthetic material, with wood still being the most popular choice. Most cheaper wooden bows use brazilwood; more expensive bows are made of pernambuco.

Brazil or pernambuco
Wooden bows that cost around fifty to two hundred dollars are almost always made of brazilwood. If you pay more, you'll get pernambuco (sometimes spelled as fernambuco), a slightly reddish type of wood. Pernambuco bows can last more than a hundred years and still play as well as when they were new.

Around two hundred
So, for around two hundred dollars you can buy an 'expensive' brazilwood bow or a cheap pernambuco bow. If two bows cost the same, choose the one that suits you and your instrument best—whichever type of wood it's made of.

Synthetic bow
Instead of wood, the stick may be made of a synthetic material—carbon fiber or fiberglass, for example. The

cheapest models, available for fifty dollars or even less, are designed mainly for children. These bows are very durable and don't need much care or attention. Professional synthetic bows are also available, and they can cost thousands of dollars.

Synthetic hair

Low-priced bows often come with synthetic hair. This provides less grip than the traditional horsehair, and it'll never make the instrument sound its best.

The mountings

A bow's *mountings* are its metal parts, such as the screw button, the *back plate* of the frog, and the *ferrule* or *D-ring*, where the bow hair enters the frog. The material used for the mounting often indicates the price and quality of the bow.

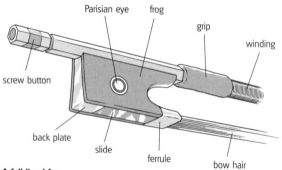

A full-lined frog.

Silver, gold, and nickel silver

Silver-mounted bows start at around three hundred and fifty or four hundred dollars, and gold-mounted bows easily cost five times as much. Cheaper pernambuco bows are usually nickel silver-mounted.

Contrary to what you might expect, nickel silver does not contain silver. The alloy is also known as *German silver* or *alpaca*.

Full-lined

The frog in the picture above is a *full-lined frog*. A *half-lined* frog does not have the back plate behind the slide or extending underneath to the slide.

Fractional-sized bows

Of course, you can also buy smaller bows for smaller violins, in similar fractional sizes. They are usually brazilwood or synthetic bows.

Viola bows

Because violas are larger, you'd expect viola bows to be longer—but they're not. In fact, viola bows are often about 0.2" (5 mm) shorter than violin bows. Even so, they are heavier: A lighter bow wouldn't get the strings of a viola to vibrate enough.

CLOSE UP

Of course, there is more to a bow than the type of wood used and the mountings—the shape of the stick, for one thing, and the decorations on and around the frog.

Eight-sided or round

The stick, *bow stick*, or *shaft*, which gets gradually thinner from the frog to the head, can be round or octagonal (eight-sided). Some violinists feel that an octagonal stick makes a bow play better, as they may be a little stiffer or more stable than round sticks.

A little more

A bow with an octagonal stick usually costs a little more than one with a round stick—not because it's necessarily better, but simply because it takes more work to make one.

Frog

The frog, which is named after a part of a horse's hoof with the same shape, is usually made of ebony. Cheap sticks sometimes have plastic frogs. The slide, at the bottom of the frog, usually has a mother-of-pearl finish. The frog itself is often decorated with single or Parisian eyes; intricately carved and decorated models are also available.

Screw button

The screw button is often inlaid. Expensive sticks may have costlier decorations, sometimes with single or Parisian eyes on each side of the octagonal screw button.

Screw buttons also come in two- and three-part versions (*i.e.*, silver-ebony, and silver-ebony-silver respectively).

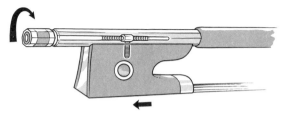

This is how you move the frog by turning the screw button.

Branded name
Usually the make of the bow or the name of the maker or the brand is literally branded into the wood of the stick, just above the frog.

Bow grip
The leather bow grip or *thumb grip* may be a little thinner on one stick than the next, and occasionally it has tiny 'ventilation holes.' Instead of leather, vinyl is sometimes used on less expensive bows. This may feel a little sticky when you play. If the bow grip feels too thin, you can install a thumb cushion, which simply slides over it. If it's too thick, its best to ask your violin maker or technician to replace it.

Winding
Silver thread is usually used for the winding or *lapping*. Some bows have a silk winding or synthetic imitation baleen windings in one or two colors. The use of real baleen (whalebone) has been banned.

Head
In the past, the protective *face* at the other end of the stick was usually made of ivory. Today, bow makers use a synthetic material, metal, or bone.

THE BEST BOW
How much should a bow cost, and which one is the best? There are no straightforward answers to either of these questions.

The price

Some violinists say your bow should cost as much as your violin. Others say half as much, or a quarter—so that's not much help. Your best bow is the one you feel most comfortable with and that helps you to make your instrument sound its best, for a price you can afford.

Suitable

Which bow suits you best depends on your bowing technique and on the music you are playing. A bow must suit your instrument too, and the strings you are using—so always try out bows with the instrument you are playing.

More expensive

As with violins, a more expensive bow is not always better, and an antique bow will often cost a lot more than an equally good new one. You can also get lucky and find a great bow for a bargain price. Even top violinists may have a 'cheap' bow in their collection because it's perfect for certain pieces of music.

Suit the music

Again, the bow should suit the style of music you play. Violinists often use a different bow for older music, say from the Baroque era, than for more recent works. Typically, they will own a variety of bows. Some bows are better for a bright, clear tone; other bows are preferable when the music requires a mellow timbre.

CHOOSING A BOW

When you've tried out ten bows in a row, you'll have forgotten what the first one sounded and played like—just like violins. It's often easier if you concentrate on, say, three bows, after a first rough selection. Reject the one you like least, then take another one to compare the other two with. And so on. First play short, simple pieces, or even just scales, and play longer pieces when you have just a few bows left to choose from.

What to play

Of course, the best test for any bow is to play the music

you intend to use it for. Try out all the bowing styles you know. Play slowly, fast, loudly, and softly, and keep listening and feeling how the bow performs. Some bows respond better to the way you play and to where exactly you bow the strings than other models—again, just like violins.

Sound

A different bow will make you sound different, just like another instrument. Brighter or warmer, heavier or lighter, fuller or thinner, softer or louder... In fact, there are even small differences between every two 'identical' bows—especially if they're wood models. These nuances will often come out best if you play slow phrases, and you'll hear more of them when playing bows and instruments in the higher price ranges.

Curved
Tipcode VIOLIN-007

A bow should be curved so that the hair, when slack, just touches the middle of the stick. If the stick is more curved than that, the hair may touch it when playing. Such bows can also feel a little restless or jumpy. A bow that is too straight, on the other hand, may be sluggish. Looking on the bright side, you could also say that a more curved bow is good for *spiccato* (in which the bow bounces lightly off the strings), while a fairly straight bow would be better for slower phrases. But then, a really good bow should allow you to play anything...

Flexibility

If you take a bow by both ends and bend it carefully, you can feel how flexible or elastic it is. A very flexible bow can make it difficult to play fast pieces, but it may have a better tone than a stiffer model. Playing may be easier with a less flexible bow, but producing a good, long tone may become trickier. And again, a good bow should allow you to play anything you can. A tip: There are synthetic bows whose flexibility can be adjusted to match your technique or the music you play.

Weight

A full-sized bow usually weighs between 2 and 2.3 ounces (55–65 grams). If you're looking for a full-bodied sound, you may want to find a relatively heavy bow. Lighter bows are often better suited for a lighter sound. If a bow is too light, it won't make the strings vibrate enough and you won't produce much sound at all.

Small
Even the smallest weight differences can influence how you sound and play. Some musicians can spot the tiniest weight differences between two bows.

Balance
The heavier a bow is at the head end, the heavier it will feel. To check its balance, make sure the hair is slack. Hold the bow between your thumb and forefinger, at about ten inches (24.5 cm) from the end of the stick itself, not including the screw button. If the head goes down, you're holding a top-heavy bow.

Top-heavy
A top-heavy stick may be easier to guide. A stick with the weight further back feels lighter, but you have to guide it more.

Response
With some bows, the tone builds up very gently and gradually, and with others the strings respond very quickly. To check the response of a bow, play lots of short notes on the lowest strings. Most violinists like to have a bow with an even response—in other words, a bow that produces the same response from the strings in the middle, near the head, and near the frog.

In line
Look along the back of the bow, from the frog, to check that it is straight. Just like a violin neck, the bow must not look as though someone has tried to wring it out.

Secondhand bows
A few tips if you're planning to buy a used bow:
- If the hair is **overstretched**, a bow will feel very sluggish. The solution is to have the bow rehaired (see page 95).
- Another problem with overstretched bow hair is that the frog needs to be shifted **very far back**. This changes the balance of the stick.

- A bow can **lose some of its curve** or *camber* over the years. It may be possible to restore it, but be sure you know whether your bow is worth the expense.
- What Stradivarius is to the violin, **François Tourte** (France, 1747-1835) is to the bow. If you find his name on a bow, it probably won't be a real Tourte, unless it has a price tag of fifty thousand dollars or more.

Brands

A few well-known bow brands are Arcos Brasil, Ary-France, Dörfler, Höfner, Paesold, Seifert, Student Arpège, Roger, Werner, and W.R. Schuster. Low-cost synthetic bows are made by Schaller, Glasser, and other companies; Berg, Coda, and Spiccato make more expensive and professional synthetic bows too.

Small

There are also dozens of small bow workshops worldwide, especially in Germany and France, where bows from around two hundred dollars and more are made. Bows by independent makers, who work alone, typically start at around a thousand dollars. If a bow doesn't have a brand name at all, it's likely a very cheap one.

ROSIN

Rosin makes the bow hair slightly sticky so it can properly 'grab' the strings and make them vibrate. When you play a string, the rosin makes it stick to the bow hair—until the tension gets too high as you move the bow along. At that point, the bow hair lets the string slip for a split second. This *stick-slip motion* is what makes the string vibrate.

Many stories

String players often use the same type of rosin for years, but experimenting a bit can't hurt. A tip in advance: There are many stories about the differences and similarities of rosins, usually contradicting one another. Trying rosins out yourself is the best thing you can do.

Hard

Each rosin cake comes wrapped in a cloth or in a box so you're less likely to touch the rosin itself. Rosin is not only sticky, but also quite hard. As a rule, a cake will easily last you a year or longer, unless you drop it: Being as hard as it is, there's a good chance it'll break.

Light and dark

Many companies sell rosins in two colors, at the same price: a light, honey-like color, and a darker color, almost like licorice. You often read that light rosins are harder and less sticky (so you should use these in the summer, when the higher temperature will make them softer). This may be true of some brands, but it can be the other way around just as well. Often, only the color is different. When you start playing, that difference vanishes as well: Rosin dust is always white.

Rosin is sold in cloths and boxes, rectangular or round blocks, and in various colors.

Harder and softer

The rosin of one brand may be harder than that of another, and some brands sell rosin in different hardnesses. You may be able to feel the difference between the softer and harder types by pressing your fingernail into them.

The best rosin?

Even experts don't agree on which rosin to choose. A few examples of their differing opinions? Softer rosin makes your strings respond better, but because it is stickier, it's more likely to produce unwanted noises. You are less likely to get those unwanted noises if you use steel strings. On the other hand, rosin developed for steel strings is often harder than rosin designed for gut strings, supposedly because gut strings don't respond properly if you use a very hard rosin…

Loud music, hard rosin?

Some experts—musicians as well as rosin makers—say that harder rosins are especially suitable for louder music, or when a fast response is required, or when the music you play requires a lot of bow pressure. However, other experts recommend harder types of rosin for quiet pieces; being less sticky, they would produce less unwanted noise.

Sticky

An extra-sticky rosin tends to produce less dust, so less gets onto your instrument. What's more, you won't need to apply as much pressure on your bow. On the other hand, this type of rosin is more likely to clog up your bow hair, which will then have to be cleaned more often. Some more expensive rosins, having finer particles, are said to produce more—and finer—dust.

Barely noticeable

Many experts believe the biggest difference between the many types of rosin is the amount of dust they produce during application and just afterwards: Once you are playing, the differences are barely noticeable, if at all. Most experts agree that this is even more true if you use a student or intermediate bow.

Confusing

Just to add to the confusion, the very same rosin is sometimes sold with a different package, label, price, and description. And while some manufacturers sell different rosins for violin, viola, and cello, others make just one for all three instruments—and some even produce special types of rosin for electric string instruments.

Gold and silver

Rosins often cost between five and fifteen dollars, including varieties that contain gold or silver particles. The precious metal is said to add clarity and brightness to the sound—but not all players can tell this subtle difference.

New bow or strings

If you buy a new bow you may well need a different rosin to do it justice, and the same is true if you start using a different type of strings. Some manufacturers try to make it easier for you to match the right strings with the right rosin by producing a rosin with the same name as each of their string series. This can be useful, though it doesn't mean that it isn't worth experimenting with other brands and types too.

Hours

Unfortunately, trying out rosins is a slow process: The old rosin will still be effective for several hours of playing after you've applied a new one. That's why violinists who use different rosins for different styles of music also have a different bow for each type of rosin—or a different type of rosin for each bow…

Non-allergenic rosin

If you're allergic to traditional rosin, try one of the hypo-allergenic or non-allergenic rosins available, or try a rosin that produces less dust. A hypo-allergenic rosin is less likely to cause a reaction, and non-allergenic rosins should not cause an allergic reaction at all.

8. FITTINGS, MUTES, AND CASES

Your two most important accessories are a properly fitting chin rest and a comfortable shoulder rest. Some of the other main accessories for your instrument are mutes and cases.

Apart from chin rests and shoulder rests, the violin's fittings or trim also include pegs and tailpieces, which were dealt with in Chapter 5, pages 38–41 and 41–42 respectively.

Chin rests

The chin rest was not widely used until about a hundred and fifty years ago. Older violins may show a lighter shade in that area, where the chins of former owners have worn away most of the varnish.

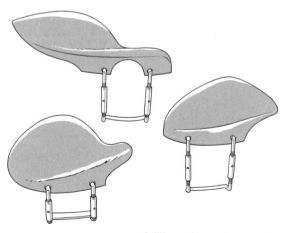

A different chin rest for every chin.

The shape of your chin

Whether you need a big chin rest or a small one, a deep one or a flat one, largely depends on the shape of your chin. Chin rests vary in height too.

Beside or above

Also, you can choose a chin rest that sits right above the tailpiece, or next to it, or somewhere in between; some rests allow you to make that choice. The closer the chin rest is to the tailpiece, the more your violin will be in line with your body when you play, and vice versa.

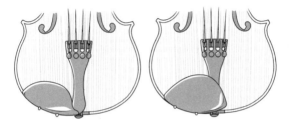

Chin rests in different positions.

Names

Chin rests usually bear the name of their designers, but they're named after cities too, or after famous violin makers (some of whom were long dead when the chin rest was invented…).

Plastic, ebony, jacaranda

Many models are available in different materials. You may find a plastic version of a certain model for less then ten dollars, while the same model in wood can cost five times as much. Expensive chin rests, selling for fifty dollars or more, are usually made of costlier woods, such as ebony, rosewood, boxwood, or jacaranda.

Wood or synthetic

If you perspire rather heavily, a wooden chin rest will probably be more comfortable than a synthetic one. If a wooden chin rest irritates your skin, you'll probably be better off with a synthetic version. If you don't know whether it is the wood, the varnish, or something else that's causing the problem, try using a cotton cloth over the chin rest for a while—some violinists always play that way. You can also buy chin rests with a soft, leather pad. Some people think they're great, others find that they get too hot for comfort.

Nickel

If you develop a rash, it may also be that you're allergic to the (nickel or nickel-plated) metal fittings of the chin rest. Special non-allergenic chin rests are available.

Match your violin

Many violinists prefer a chin rest that matches the type and color of the tailpiece, and of course goes with the rest of the violin. If you do too, it's worth knowing that you can buy ready-made sets with a chin rest, a tailpiece, tuning pegs, and even an end button in the same color and style.

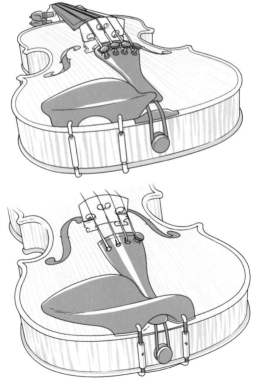

The chin rest may be attached to the left of the end button, or using one clamp on either side.

Two clamps

Most chin rests attach to the instrument with two clamps. You can tighten or loosen them with a paper clip, but a special chin rest wrench or key helps to prevent damaging the body. Some chin rests can be set with screws.

Where

Both clamps can be attached to the left of the end button, or there's a clamp on either side. The latter type may be preferred as this places the clamps close to the bottom block—the small wooden block that holds the end button (see page 115).

Too tight, too loose

A chin rest only touches the violin at the edges. To prevent damage, its clamps are covered with cork. If a chin rest is put on too tight, you risk deforming the ribs, or even the plates. If it's too loose, it could slip off.

Small and large

Of course, there are special chin rests for fractional-sized violins and for violas. In both cases, there is slightly less choice.

SHOULDER REST

The shoulder rest is an even more recent invention than the chin rest. It has only been widely used since the 1950s, and it's still frowned upon by some.

Higher

Using a shoulder rest means that your instrument will sit a little higher on your shoulder, so you don't have to tilt your head as far to the left. On the other hand, you do need to lift your right arm higher, which sometimes causes pain or other symptoms. A lower type of shoulder rest together with a higher chin rest can help avoid such problems.

Pads and wooden rests

Some violinists still prefer the simplest shoulder rest of all: a small cushion or pad, or even a special sponge, the latter selling for no more than a couple of dollars. Others use the traditional wooden shoulder rest, covered with cloth and held in place with rubber bands.

Wide variety

Shoulder pads come in a wide variety of shapes and materials, attached with rubber bands, leather straps or a combination of both. If you have a long neck, go for a slightly larger model. Also available are inflatable cushions, so you can decide yourself how thick and hard it should be.

Damage

Note that the materials used for some pads or cushions can damage certain types of violin varnish. Sounds pretty vague indeed—so ask your violin maker or dealer for advice.

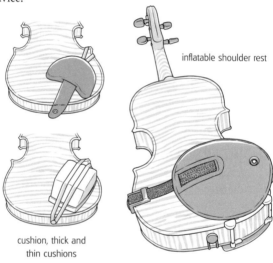

inflatable shoulder rest

cushion, thick and
thin cushions

Bridge

Some violinists dislike pads or sponges, which they believe muffle the vibrations of the back of the instrument. In reality, however, hardly anyone can really hear the difference. In case of doubt: There are pads that are mounted on a 'bridge,' so they don't touch the body of the violin. This also prevents damaging or wearing the varnish.

Fingers

The most popular shoulder rests consist of a wooden,

plastic, or metal bar, covered with soft sponge rubber, which spans the back of the violin like a bridge. This type of shoulder rest is attached with four *fingers*, which should adjust to perfectly fit your instrument. A tip: Check now and again to see if the soft protective tubing of the fingers hasn't worn out, which would expose the finish and the wood of your violin to the metal underneath.

Height-adjustable

Some shoulder rests are also height-adjustable, on some the bar can be bent to perfectly fit your shoulders, and there are special shoulder rests available for musicians with wider or narrower shoulders. Non-adjustable models often come in two or more heights.

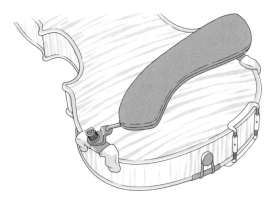

An adjustable shoulder rest.

Attach and remove

Unlike chin rests, shoulder rests are supposed to be taken off the violin when it's not being played, so try out different shoulder rests to see how easy they are to attach and remove. Some models are collapsible so that they fit in your case more easily.

Brands

Examples of well-known brands of shoulder rests are Johnson, Kadenza, Kun, Menuhin, Viva la Musica, and Wolf. Some brands offer shoulder rests in bright colors, alongside the many models with a traditional appearance. Fully adjustable shoulder rests are available from twenty or twenty-five dollars.

MUTES

If you place a *mute* on the bridge of your instrument, the sound becomes softer, mellower or warmer: Mutes muffle some of the higher frequencies of the sound. If the composer wants you to use a mute, the score will show the instruction 'with mute' in Italian: *con sordino*. Practice mutes (see page 16) muffle the sound a lot more than regular mutes do. A wolf tone eliminator (see below) is yet another type of mute, with a very specific purpose.

Clothing pin

As discussed on pages 35–36, a heavy bridge will slightly muffle the sound of your instrument. A mute works in pretty much the same way, as it simply adds mass to the bridge. The bigger or heavier a mute is, the more it will muffle the sound, the added mass absorbing the vibrations. Want to try it out? Very carefully attach a wooden clothing pin to the bridge of your instrument, and you'll hear that the sound will be muffled slightly. If you attach another clothing pin, doubling the added mass, the muffling effect will be even stronger.

Variety

Mutes come in rubber, metal, or wood, and in a wide variety of models. Most mutes are very affordable, often costing under five dollars.

Detachable or slide-on

The most basic mute, a three-pronged model, looks like a short, thick comb. You only put it onto your instrument when you need it. Another type, the *fixed mute* or *slide-on*

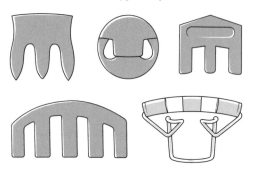

Various mutes, some looking like short, thick combs...

mute, stays attached to your strings. If you don't need it, you slide it over toward the tailpiece. Slide-on mutes come in rubber (i.e., the Tourte model) and wire versions.

Which one

Slide-on mutes are especially easy if a composition requires you to alternately play with and without a mute. However, some players rather not use one because, even when it's at the tailpiece, a clip-on mute could muffle the sound (though you're unlikely to hear the difference), or because it might vibrate along with the strings, causing noise. Other musicians thoroughly dislike the other type of mutes (*clip-on mutes*) as they get lost so easily.

A tiny bit

A wire mute can be used to make your sound just a tiny bit sweeter. To do so, slide it to a position somewhere between

A slide-on wire mute at the tailpiece...

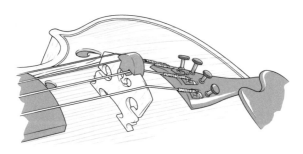

... and a rubber slide-on mute (Tourte) on the bridge.

the bridge and the tailpiece. The closer you get to the bridge, the stronger the muffling effect. You can also set a wire mute diagonally, so that it muffles the high strings more than the low ones, or the other way around.

Wolf tone

Occasionally, a violin will produce a *wolf tone*—a stuttering sound, somewhat like a howling wolf. You can usually put an end to this problem with a *wolf tone eliminator*, a metal tube that is attached to the relevant string between bridge and tailpiece, wherever it has the greatest effect. Wolf tones are more common on cellos than on violins and violas.

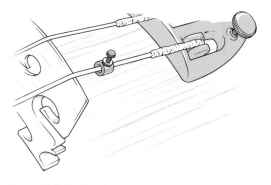

A wolf tone eliminator in action.

CASES

Except for low-budget instruments, most violins and violas come without a case—so usually you have to buy this essential protection separately.

Oblong or violin-shaped

Cases are available in a variety of styles. Oblong cases usually have one or more accessory pockets to store your shoulder rest, a set of spare strings, mutes, and rosin. *Shaped cases*, of which the outline vaguely resembles a violin, have less room for accessories.

Shell and covering

Most cases have a hard shell, made of plywood or plastic synthetic material (*i.e.*, thermoplastic, ABS) covered with either vinyl, cloth, or leather.

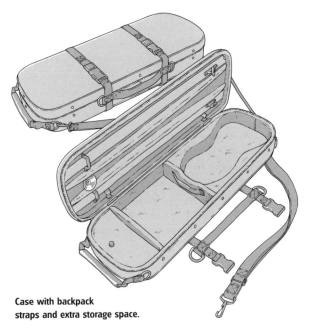

**Case with backpack
straps and extra storage space.**

Case covers

A violin case must be waterproof, so check that it really closes properly. Cases with a cloth, canvas, Cordura, or nylon cover often have a separate flap that goes across the opening. Separate case covers are also available, often with an extra pocket for sheet music. On some models, the case cover can be screwed to the case.

Locks

Most cases are lockable. This is mainly to ensure that the catches cannot open by accident—for instance, if you drop your case—so make it a habit to always lock them.

Locks and hinges

When choosing a case, check the locks, hinges, handles, and carrying straps carefully: Usually, these are the weak spots.

A good case

A good case offers substantial shock absorption, and it's sturdy enough to resist being crushed as long as things don't get too extreme. The cheapest cases, with less padding and weaker cores, may not offer enough protection.

Two to six pounds
The lightest cases weigh only two pounds, whereas heavy models may weigh three times as much. Very light models are usually less shockproof than heavier ones. Incidentally, the violin itself weighs about a pound.

Inside
Many cases have a Velcro strip to hold the neck in place. It will also stop your violin from falling out, should you accidentally open the case the wrong way up. A case also should have a soft, plush-lined interior to absorb shocks and prevent scratches. The padding tends to be thicker in more expensive cases. If a choice between a velour or a velvet lining is offered, the latter will cost a little extra.

Suspension cases
In a suspension case, the instrument is literally suspended: Being a little deeper at the back and the scroll of the instrument, these vulnerable parts will not touch the bottom of the case.

Bow holders
The inside of the lid usually has holders (*bow slots*) for two or sometimes three bows. A tip: Always put the bows in with their hair facing outwards. Separate bow cases are also available, for one or more bows.

Protective cloth
To prevent the bows from damaging or contaminating (rosin!) the instrument, cover the instrument with a cloth before closing the case. Some cases come with a cloth or a foam pad for that purpose. Instead of a cloth, you can use a bag. Many players prefer a silk one.

String tube
Cases always have room for spare strings. If you use gut strings, which should not be rolled up, you need a special *string tube*.

Backpack straps
If you don't drive, carrying your violin will be easier if your case has removable, adjustable backpack straps, or at least a shoulder strap.

Smaller and bigger

Because violas vary in size, viola cases come in different sizes too. The more expensive models are often adjustable. Some violin and viola cases come with a removable insert, so you can use the same case for instruments in various sizes. If you play violin as well as viola, you can get a case that holds both, and there are even cases that hold four instruments.

Prices

Expect to pay at least a hundred dollars for a case that can really take a knock, but you can get cheaper ones too, starting around fifty dollars. The most luxurious, leather-lined cases easily cost ten times as much.

Hygrometer

Violins are particularly sensitive to very dry air. Some of the more expensive cases available have a built-in hygrometer, so you can check humidity at any time (see pages 105–106).

Violin stands

If you take a short break, it may be easy to have a padded violin stand handy, rather than putting the violin back in its case or laying it down somewhere. Violin stands, available for around fifty dollars, usually have a holder for the bow too.

9. ELECTRIC VIOLINS

If you play your violin in a band, you're likely to find that it isn't loud enough. Rather than use a regular microphone, you can get yourself a ready-made electric violin, or turn your classical instrument into an electric one, or attach a clip-on microphone to it. Electric violins can also be used to practice in complete silence, using headphones.

Basically, there are two types of electric violins: The ones that hardly produce any sound at all when unamplified, and regular violins that have been converted to electric ones. The latter can be played unamplified (*i.e.*, acoustically) as well, so they're really acoustic/electric instruments.

Acoustic/electric violins

Converting a regular violin to an electric one is done by supplying it with one or two *pickups* or *transducers*. These

Violin with a pickup in the bridge (Fishman).

small, flat 'sensors' literally pick up the vibrations of the strings, and convert them to electric signals that can be amplified.

Between wings and feet
Most violin pickups are wedged between the bridge wings and feet, or under the feet. Because your bridge will usually need some filing for a good fit, and because the precise positioning is very important to the sound, it's best to let an expert install them for you. Alternatively, you can get a pickup that sticks to the bridge with adhesive.

Preamplifier
The signals produced by most pickups need to be boosted before they're sent to the main amplifier. In ready-made electric violins, the required preamplifier is usually built into the instrument, and so are its controls (*e.g.*, volume and tone). If you install a pickup on a regular violin, you can attach the preamp to your clothing or your belt. Also, there are systems that have their controls in a chin rest style device.

Output
The output for the instrument cable is usually mounted on the side of the instrument, or on its tailpiece. Some systems have a standard ¼" phone jack output; others use a smaller (3.5 mm), lighter mini jack.

Feedback
Using pickups, you can play really loud without to much risk of being bothered by feedback—the loud screech you also hear if you point a microphone at a loudspeaker. However, pickups can make your instrument sound less warm and natural than a microphone would.

Clip-on microphone
That's why some violinists prefer to use a miniature clip-on microphone—which has the drawback of making the instrument more sensitive to feedback. Clip-on microphones need a preamp too.

Both worlds
A best-of-both-worlds solution is to use a pickup as well

as a (vocal) microphone on a stand, or to buy a set that features both a pickup and a clip-on mic. A control sets the balance between the two. You use just the microphone if timbre is what counts and the required volume is low enough not to cause feedback, or just the pickup if you're playing with a really loud band, or a mix of the two. Yet another alternative is a bridge-mounted microphone that has the sound characteristics of a microphone but looks like a pickup, and that behaves like a pickup when it comes to resisting feedback.

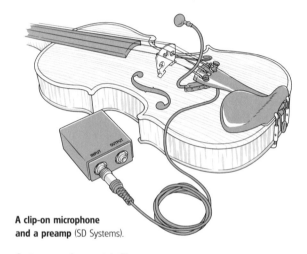

**A clip-on microphone
and a preamp** (SD Systems).

Cotton wool or notch filter

Even when using pickups on your 'regular' violin, feedback can occur. A basic trick to fight feedback is to fill the body of your instrument with bits of cotton wool, which can later be removed with a crotchet needle. (Take care not to touch the sound post!) A more sophisticated solution is to use a (pre)amp with a *notch filter*, which combats feedback by filtering the relevant frequency out of the sound.

Prices and brands

You can buy a decent violin pickup for as little as seventy-five dollars, and sometimes even less, but you can spend a lot more too: Systems with both a pickup and a mic can easily set you back some five hundred dollars. Some well-known companies in this field include Barcus Berry, B-band, Bowtronics, Fishman, L.R. Baggs, Schaller, SD Systems, Seymour Duncan, and Shadow.

Solid-body violins

Electric violins that are designed to be played 'electric only' come in many different shapes. Some still have the basic outline of the traditional instrument; others have solid bodies in Z-, S- or V-shaped designs, the latter sometimes being hardly recognizable as a violin.

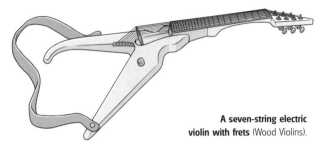

A seven-string electric violin with frets (Wood Violins).

Frets and seven strings

These instruments have all sorts of other options as well. For example, there are electric violins with a fretted neck (like a guitar), and you can get them with five, six or seven strings. The extra strings are all tuned to lower pitches than the regular violin's G.

Practice in silence

Solid-body electric violins can be used for silent practice too. The best-known example of an instrument that was designed specifically for that purpose is Yamaha's Silent Violin (see page 17). It features a small built-in amplifier for a pair of headphones, and there's an input to connect a CD, MD or cassette player to the instrument, allowing you to play along with pre-recorded music. Also, it has a built-in reverb to add some extra life to the sound. Of course, the instrument can be amplified as well.

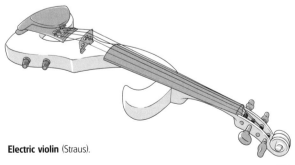

Electric violin (Straus).

Prices and brands

Electric violins are available from around three hundred to more than three thousand dollars. Some of the companies that make solid-body violins are Dal, T.F. Barrett, Bridge, Fender (the guitar makers), Fidelius, Jordan, Skyinbow, Straus, TB, Wood, and Zeta. Ready-made acoustic/electric instruments are available from Barcus-Berry, Importuno, Meisel, Palatino, and others.

MIDI

Some electric violins can be hooked up to synthesizers, effect devices, computers, and other digital equipment. For this purpose, they feature MIDI, a standardized *musical instrument digital interface.*

Amplification

If you play electric, you can either use the band's or the venue's PA system, or you can buy your own amplifier. Most violinists use a special type of amp that is designed to be used for acoustic instruments, known as—believe it or not—an *acoustic amplifier.* They're usually combo amplifiers, with one or more relatively small loudspeakers and an amplifier all in one box, often featuring one or more effects such as reverb or chorus. Some players prefer a regular guitar amp (designed for electric guitars) instead. For more information, please consult *Tipbook Amplifiers and Effects* (see page 131).

10. TUNING

A violin has to be tuned before you can play it. When you start out your teacher will tune it for you, but sooner or later you'll have to do it yourself. Is it difficult? No, but you'll only learn properly by doing it often. This chapter offers basic information and helpful hints.

A violin won't easily go out of tune if it's in good condition. Even so, you always need to check the tuning before you start playing. If you have them, fine tuners are usually all you need to adjust the tuning.

Tuning pegs   Tipcode VIOLIN-008

It is hard to tune synthetic strings and—even moreso— steel strings with the tuning pegs only: Even the slightest rotation of a peg translates into a major difference in the tension on the string. If you're not careful, you even can easily tighten a string so much that it breaks.

Fine tuners

That's why synthetic and steel strings usually have fine tuners. The large tuning pegs are used only to roughly 'pretune' the strings. When doing so, make sure the fine tuners are in their middle settings, so you can use them to tune up as well as down.

Plucking or bowing?

You can sound the string you are tuning by plucking, as you would with a guitar. For beginners that's easier, but you can hear what you're doing better if you bow the strings. Before you can do either, you'll have to learn how to hold your violin under your chin while you bow or pluck with your right hand, and operate the fine tuners or pegs with your left.

Tuning as you bow...

The pitches
The strings of a violin and viola are tuned to the following pitches:

	Violin	Viola	
String 1	E	A	(thinnest, highest sounding string)
String 2	A	D	
String 3	D	G	
String 4	G	C	(thickest, lowest sounding string)

The A
Most orchestral instruments are tuned to the A that sounds the same pitch as the A-string of a well-tuned violin or viola.

A=440
If a string sounds at this pitch, it is vibrating at 440 times per second. This pitch is usually referred to as A=440 hertz or simply A=440 (see page 12).

Piano
The A-string is the first string to tune. You can match this string to that A on the piano that sounds the same pitch: This would be the A to the right of Middle C, called A4 (again, see page 12).

Pedal
If you use a piano, press the right pedal down and then play the A-key. This will make the note sound for a long

time, which makes it easier to use for reference as you tune your violin.

Tuning fork   Tipcode VIOLIN-009

If you don't have a piano handy, you can buy a tuning fork—a thick, two-pronged metal fork. Tap it on your knee, hold the stem against or near your ear, and you'll hear the A. Also, the A=440 can be played back on many electronic metronomes and electronic tuners, and you can find it as an audio sample at www.tipbook.com.

A=442

Some orchestras tune to an A that is a tiny bit higher. You can buy tuning forks for these tunings too, such as A=442.

Tuning fork.

Too high, too low?   Tipcode VIOLIN-006

The first string you tune is always the A. Listen to the reference pitch A and turn the fine tuner until the string sounds that same pitch. In the beginning, it can be difficult to hear whether a string is too high or too low. Here's a trick: First turn the fine tuner of the relevant string all the way down. Then you can be almost certain that its pitch is *flat* (too low). From there, slowly bring the pitch up.

Singing

You can also sing along. First listen closely to the reference pitch and sing it. Then sing the pitch the string is making. Usually, you will then 'feel' if you have to sing higher or lower, and you can adjust the string accordingly.

In the middle

If you start with the fine tuners in their middle settings, you can typically tune each string up or down a whole tone or even more. In most cases, this is enough to get them to the correct pitches.

The E
Tipcode VIOLIN-010

Once the A is right, tune the E-string. You can find this E on a piano too (E5), but you can also do it without one. Try singing the first two words of *Twinkle, Twinkle, Little Star*. If you sing the first *Twinkle* at the same pitch as your A-string, the second *Twinkle* will be at the pitch your E-string should have.

Perfect fifth

The 'distance' or *interval* from the first to the second *Twinkle* is referred to as a *perfect fifth*.

Backwards
Tipcode VIOLIN-011 and VIOLIN-012

On violins and violas, all adjacent strings are a perfect fifth apart. To tune a lower sounding string to a higher sounding string, you should sing the first two 'Twinkles' backwards: Sing the second *Twinkle* while playing the higher sounding string, and match the lower sounding string to the first, lower sounding *Twinkle*.

G and D

This way, you can tune the D-string to the A-string, and then tune the G to the D.

Viola

On a viola you also begin with the A-string, of course. From there go to the D, the G, and finally the C. The interval between each pair of strings, again, is a perfect fifth.

Check

When you have tuned all four strings, check them once more. Usually you'll have to adjust the tuning here or there. The nursery rhyme will point you in the right direction, but there is a better way to hear whether the instrument is in tune.

Better still
Tipcode VIOLIN-013

The trick is to bow two adjacent strings. Again, a perfectly tuned A string is your reference. If the sound of any pair of strings is slightly wavey, carefully adjust the second string. The slower the waves or 'beats' get, the closer you are. When they're gone, the string pair is in tune, so proceed to the next pair.

Careful

If you are adjusting your fine tuners as you bow, there's a good chance you'll press them down slightly without meaning to. This pressure will make the string's pitch go up. So as soon as you let go of the fine tuner, the pitch will drop, and you'll have to start again. The solution? First adjust the string, then let go of the fine tuner and listen— and so on.

Bowing

When you're tuning, try to make sure you bow with a consist, light pressure. If you don't, the tuning may turn out to be less than perfect as soon as you start playing.

With a piano

You can of course tune all your strings with the relevant keys of a piano, but you'll learn to tune better if you tune from the A-string. After all, that's how you'll often have to do it if you play in an orchestra or in another group or ensemble.

Pitch pipe

Pitch pipes are popular tuning aids. There are two types, those with one note (the A) and those with four (one for each string). Pitch pipes are cheap, but they tend to go out of tune quickly. Besides, it's easier to compare your A-string with a tuning fork.

Chromatic tuner

An electronic *chromatic* tuner tells you exactly which pitch it is hearing, and whether it is *flat* (too low), *sharp* (too high), or exactly right. You can buy one for twenty-five dollars or more. They are especially popular with guitarists. Violinists often say it's better to learn to tune by ear, because you also depend on your ear to tell you whether you are playing in tune—which is less of a topic for guitarists, with their fretted instruments.

A little higher

Strings stretch as they get older. Eventually they may come to a point where your fine tuners can't get them in tune anymore. If so, you'll have to tune them a little higher with your pegs. Before you do, first loosen the string with the fine tuner as far as it will go. Tip: If a string has been stretched this far, chances are it needs to be replaced.

Tuning with pegs Tipcode VIOLIN-008

When you use the pegs, it's easiest if you tune upwards: If a string sounds sharp, first turn the peg until it's flat and then go back up from there. Apart from that, tuning with pegs is really the same as tuning with fine tuners—though it may take some time to learn how to adjust them.

Scordatura

Very occasionally, violins are tuned differently. For example, the pitch of the lowest string might be reduced by a whole tone or a half-tone (half-step). Such alternative tunings are known as *scordatura*.

11. VIOLIN MAINTENANCE

Real repairs and violin adjustment are best left to an expert. But there is plenty you can do yourself to keep your instrument in the best possible condition: cleaning, replacing strings, straightening the bridge, finding buzzes, and much more.

The rosin from your bow lands on your violin as dust. You can easily wipe most of it off with a soft, lint-free cloth each time you finish playing. A cotton cloth will do fine; an old, unprinted T-shirt for instance, or a dishcloth. With older instruments especially, watch out for splinters around the edges. Don't forget to clean the bow stick too. On some finishes (*e.g.*, synthetic finishes) you can use a slightly damp cloth as well, if necessary.

Fingerboard and strings
It's best to use a different cloth for the neck, strings, and fingerboard, where you touch them with your fingers. Wipe the strings with the cloth and then pull it between the fingerboard and the strings. Again, a cotton cloth is good for the job, but some violinists prefer to use silk. Once you've cleaned your violin, put it back in its case.

Prevention
Strings will live longer if you wash your hands before playing, and your violin will be easier to keep clean if you only hold it by the neck and in the area of the chin rest.

Violin cleaner
Every violin needs extra attention once in a while, even if

you are very careful. The top can get sticky and dull, especially between the *f*-holes, where most of the rosin ends up. You can remove it with a special violin cleaner.

Violin polish
There are special cleaners and cleaning cloths that polish your instrument as well, smoothing away fine scratches.

The best?
Which is the best cleaner for your violin depends on its varnish, so always ask what you can and cannot use on your instrument when you buy or rent it. Before using a cleaner, always read the instructions. Then try a small area first, preferably one that's out of sight: Some delicate varnishes can be damaged by an abrasive polish, or by a cleaner that contains harsh solvents.

Never
Whatever you do, never use ordinary household cleaners. One exception would be using a window cleaner on a plastic chin rest. Do take the chin rest off first.

The fingerboard
You can occasionally give the fingerboard an extra cleaning by dabbing it with a soft cloth, moistened with some rubbing alcohol. Do make sure that no liquid gets onto the varnish of the body: Keep the bottle well out of the way and do not allow the cloth to drag over the body. For safety's sake, lay another, dry cloth over the body.

The strings
Your strings need to be cleaned from time to time, to remove rosin residue, grime, and finger oils. Take a clean cloth and push it along the strings a few times from the top of the fingerboard to the bridge. Don't push too hard, and hold one hand across the strings, because they can really screech when you do this.

Alcohol, steel wool, and string oil
If this doesn't work, you may moisten the cloth with rubbing alcohol, provided you don't use gut strings. Again, do not spill any of this liquid on the instrument. Special string cleaners are available as well, and some technicians

use very fine steel wool to remove rosin residue. Tip: Plain gut strings retain their elasticity by treating them with special string oil or almond oil.

Inside
Over the course of the years, dust and dirt will inevitably find its way inside your violin. To get it out, some violinists pour in half a handful of dry, uncooked rice and carefully shake it through the body a few times. The rice comes out again by turning the violin upside down, and carefully shaking it—which makes the rice clean the underside of the top at the same time. Most of the dust will come out with the rice.

Check
You should regularly inspect your violin for splinters or other minor damage. Also check whether the chin rest is still secure, and that the tubing of the fingers of your shoulder rest is in good shape.

Expert
There are times when you'll need to take your instrument to an expert—when it needs more extensive cleaning, if there are stains that won't go away, if you can't get the neck clean, or if the varnish is becoming very dull (on the body, under the strings, or where you touch the body with your left hand). Many musicians have their instruments checked once a year, even if nothing seems to be wrong, just to be on the safe side.

Plastic
If your sweat is especially acidic, it can damage the varnish and even the wood of the ribs where your left hand touches it. The solution? There are violin makers who stick a strip of self-adhesive plastic to the rib. Some are appalled at the very idea, others see it as simply being practical.

TUNING PEGS AND FINE TUNERS
Fine tuners do not require much maintenance, if any at all. If one does get a little stiff, you may apply a tiny bit of acid-free vaseline. Wooden tuning pegs, on the other hand, can be troublesome.

Peg compound

The tuning pegs need to be able to turn smoothly, without slipping back. If they get stuck or they slip, try using a little *peg compound* or *peg dope*. A stopgap solution for slipping pegs is to apply white chalk, which eventually will wear out the hole. Some types of soap are used too, but soap may congeal and make tuning harder. A third alternative is to wind your strings so that they force the peg deeper into the peg hole, by letting the string wind up against the cheek of the peg box. This too is a stopgap solution: Jamming the string against the cheek may cause it to break (see page 100).

Loose

If a peg or its hole is badly worn, the peg may get really loose. Having a new set of bigger pegs custom-fit to the instrument will usually cost some fifty to a hundred dollars. This may or may not include the pegs, which vary from ten to fifty dollars for a set—but there are more expensive ones too, with golden rings or other expensive decorations. If the peg holes are really worn out, they can be *rebushed*.

BOW

Maintaining your bow comes down to applying rosin to it, keeping it clean and having it rehaired when necessary. Here are some helpful hints.

Rosin   Tipcode VIOLIN-014

Applying rosin is necessary only when the bow hair gets too smooth, probably no more than once or twice a week. Move the bow hair over the rosin cake rather than the other way around, applying the rosin along the full length of the hair, from the head to the frog. If you keep your thumb on the ferrule when you do this, it won't damage the rosin cake.

Two tips

Tip one: Prevent the bow hair from wearing a groove in the cake (creating 'walls' of unusable rosin) by rotating it now and again. Tip two: Don't touch the bow hair or the cake, as perspiration and finger oil will keep the rosin from holding on to the bow hair.

Excess rosin

Wipe the bow hair with a cloth when you have finished, or drag one of your nails across the bow hairs close to the frog. This makes sure that the excess rosin doesn't land on your violin. You can shake out your bow instead, but it's best not to: Even if you don't break anything or hit anybody, whipping can damage your bow.

Cleaning

The bow hair often gets a bit grimy near the frog. You can clean it with a lukewarm, damp cloth, possibly using a little washing-up liquid in the water. The ends of the bow hair are held in place by small wooden wedges. Be sure not to get them wet.

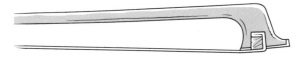

The bow hair is held in place by small wooden wedges.

Too smooth

If you need to apply rosin more and more often, that's probably due to old bow hair (have it replaced) or to a buildup of rosin residue, which makes the hair slick. Some violinists clean the hair themselves, using a cloth that's very lightly moistened with rubbing alcohol—but it is much safer to have it done by an expert. The liquid can easily damage the stick, and you may end up with the bow hair sticking together, rendering the bow unplayable. A bow maker or violin technician can decide whether cleaning will help, or if rehairing is necessary.

New hair

If the bow hair is overstretched, you can't get the bow back to proper tension. The usual solution is a rehair. A rehair typically costs some forty or fifty dollars. In some cases, the bow hair can be shortened instead. If you only play for a few hours a week, the bow hair will last for years. Good-quality hair will not become wavy or brittle.

Broken bow hair

If a hair breaks, remove the loose ends by cutting them off at the sharp edge of the ferrule or the face, rather than pulling them out. Another solution is to cut them carefully with scissors, as close as possible to the ferrule or face.

Not tight

If you can't get the hair to the desired tension, the bow hair may be overstretched, or your bow stick could be slowly loosing its curve. A bow maker or violin technician may be able to restore the curve.

Slide smoothly

If the frog doesn't slide smoothly and the end screw feels stiff, remove them by turning the end screw until it comes off. A simple cleaning will usually do. Don't use oil for screw parts. Instead, gently rub the screw on a candle. No effect? Then have the bow looked at. Do so too if the frog wobbles or if the grip needs to be replaced..

NEW STRINGS

If your strings break or if the windings come loose, you need to replace them. The same is true if they're getting old: Old strings get more and more difficult to tune, and they will sound duller and duller. The better your instrument, the better your playing, and the better your ear, the sooner you'll hear when strings need to be replaced.

How long

How long a set of strings will last you depends on many things. If you have synthetic strings and you play for a few hours a week, you might try fitting new strings after six months or so. If you hear the difference straightaway, try replacing the new set after just four months. If you can't hear any difference after six months, wait a little longer before replacing your strings next time. Your strings will always last you longer if you keep your strings and your hands clean, and if your perspiration isn't too acidic.

Longer

Steel strings usually last a bit longer than synthetic strings, and gut strings wear out the quickest. When should you replace your strings? When plucking them only produces a short, dull tone, it's a sign that they are wearing out. If they become discolored, you're also better off replacing them. Note, however, that silver-wound strings may still sound fine long after they have begun to discolor.

Wound strings

Some windings—aluminum, for instance—are easily blemished by certain types of perspiration. If this happens, try using a set of strings with a different type of winding, such as chrome-steel.

A new set

If one of your wound strings breaks, the new string you put on may sound a lot brighter than the older ones. If so, the only solution is to replace the other wound strings too. A new E-string can usually be fitted without replacing the rest. Some violinists claim their instrument sounds better if they use cheap E-strings and replace them often, rather than playing one expensive E-string for a longer period of time. A tip: Used strings can still be useful as spares.

Not more than two

Before replacing your strings, lay your violin on a folded towel, or on your lap. An important tip: Don't take off more than two strings at a time, so that the other strings keep the bridge and sound post in place. If the sound post still falls over, loosen all the strings and have it set in position by an expert.

The middle one   Tipcode VIOLIN-015

In the pegbox, the two outer strings pass below the middle ones. This makes them harder to get to. So first remove one of the middle strings, and then the string that passes below it. Now replace the outer string, and then the middle one. An example: Release the D, then the G; replace the G, then the D; proceed similarly with the other two strings.

Removing strings

To remove a string, slightly pull the peg outward and slowly turn it toward the body of the instrument. Then pull gently on the string, so the peg will start turning until the string comes loose. Guide the string between your thumb and index finger near the pegbox, so that it can't suddenly come loose and cause damage.

Cut

You can also turn the peg until the string is slack and then cut it by the pegbox. It is easier and safer to remove the remaining bit than a whole, long string, some say.

Fitting strings

Tipcode VIOLIN-016

You can fit new strings in various ways. This is one simple way.

- Turn the peg so that the hole points diagonally upwards, facing the fingerboard.
- Attach the string to the tailpiece.
- Stick the string through the peg (illustration 1) and start winding it. Make sure the hole moves in the direction of the scroll.

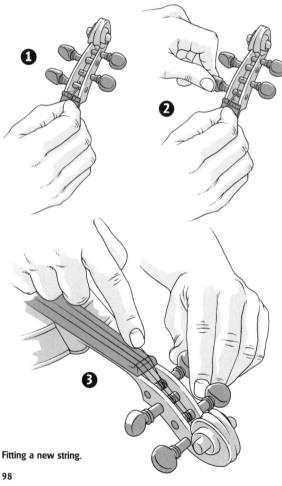

Fitting a new string.

- Hold the string with your other hand so that it can't go slack and slip out of the hole or come loose from the tailpiece (illustration 2).
- Keep tightening the string, making sure that the windings run outwards, toward the thicker end of the peg. Use your index finger to keep the string tight and to guide it through the groove in the nut (illustration 3).
- Tune it so that it is at roughly the right tension, comparing it to the strings that are still in place.

Kink

You may find that a string keeps on coming loose from the peg as you try to tighten it. If so, take a small pair of pliers and make a kink about half an inch (1–1.5 cm) from the very end of the string. The kink will make the string hook itself in place as you begin to turn the peg.

Pegs in poor condition

Making a kink in the string can also help keeping your strings in place if your pegs are in poor condition. Stick the string through the peg's hole, and then lay the kinked end flat against the peg. Let the string run over it a couple of times as you turn the peg. Please note: Do not wind the plain (non-wound) part of a wound string around itself.

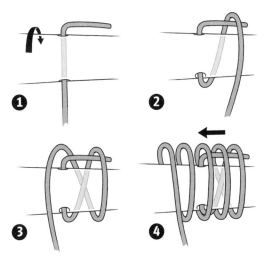

This way, the strings will always stay properly in place. Make a kink in the string, lay it against the peg, and let the unwound part of the string wind around it a couple of times.

Long string

If a string happens to be very long, you can first let it wind inwards for a few turns before guiding it back the other way. The last few turns must be wound directly onto the wood, and not on top of another part of the string. Tip: Four or five windings should be enough to prevent a string from slipping.

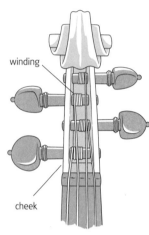

winding

cheek

Leave space between windings and cheeks.

Space

Strings can break if they are jammed against the cheeks of the pegbox. So always make sure they have some space—unless you're in trouble because of a slipping peg (see page 94).

String sleeves

If you use string sleeves (see page 55), slide them into place when the strings are nearly tuned. A sleeve does the most good on the E-string. Instead of a regular sleeve, many violinists lay a tiny piece of vellum (parchment) under the string.

Protection

A tip: There are special fine tuners for gut strings. Other types will cut through the loop of a gut string in no time. You can extend the life of your strings with E-string protectors. Some violinists even use them for steel E-strings.

The loop of a gut string.

The first time

When you are replacing a string for the first time, you'll probably find you don't have enough hands. You need one to tighten, another to make sure the string doesn't come loose from the tailpiece, a third one to guide it through the grooves in the bridge and nut... So it's handy to have someone else around.

Grooves

When you replace your strings, check the pegs at the same time. Grooves in the pegs can make your strings break. If the pegs won't grip the strings whatever you do, there's a chance that the holes are worn out.

Damage

Your strings can also be easily damaged by sharp edges on the bridge, the nut, or around the string-holes in the pegs. The grooves in the nut must be smooth and nicely rounded to prevent the strings from kinking. Check your instrument carefully if a string keeps breaking at the same point. If a string doesn't run smoothly across the nut or the bridge, twist the point of a soft pencil through the groove a few times. If that doesn't do the trick, you'll need expert help.

Perfect fifths

On a properly tuned violin or viola, there is always a perfect fifth between one open string and the next (see page 88). You can check this by laying a pencil across two strings and pressing down so that they both touch the fingerboard. In both high and low positions, the difference in pitch between the two strings should always be a perfect fifth. If you have old strings, this may not be so, perhaps because one string is more stretched than the other. If so, the first will sound flat. Old strings are not the only possible cause if you don't hear perfect fifths; the bridge may be the culprit instead. Another tip: If you use traditional gut strings, you may not hear perfect fifths either.

THE BRIDGE

The bridge is held in place by the strings. Their tension also pulls the bridge forward and pushes it down. Altogether, the bridge has to withstand around sixty pounds of pressure—so do keep an eye on it.

Perpendicular

Now and then, you should check that the bridge hasn't

started leaning forward, toward the fingerboard. You can carefully try to push it back in its original position yourself, with its back perpendicular to the violin's top, but don't hesitate to leave this to a violin maker or technician. Another check: Make sure that both feet are exactly lined up with the notches in the f-holes. If not, your instrument will not produce perfect fifths (see the previous page).

New bridge

If the downward pressure of the strings has forced the bridge to bend, you need a new one. The bridge also needs replacing if the grooves have become too deep: No more than a third of the diameter of each string should be inside the groove. If you switch to different strings, the string height may need to be adjusted. This often requires a new or modified bridge. Another reason to have your bridge changed or replaced is that it's too flat (so that you accidentally play two strings instead of one), or too curved (making it difficult to play two or three strings at once).

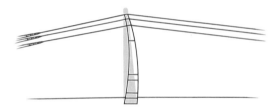

Bridge bending toward the fingerboard.

Summer and winter bridges

There are violinists who use two bridges: A higher one in the winter, as the lower humidity (see page 105) makes the wood shrink and the arching of the instrument becomes less pronounced, so that string height is reduced—and a lower one in the summer, when the reverse happens.

Custom-fit

A new bridge needs to be custom-fit to the violin, so that it has the right height and curve for the instrument, and so that its feet match the top perfectly. Having a new bridge installed will often cost between fifty and seventy-five dollars, the bridge itself being the least expensive factor. A new bridge should last for years.

More than carving alone

There are bridges with moveable feet which automatically adjust to the arch of the top—but even you prefer this type of bridge, it can't hurt to have a specialist install it: Again, properly fitting a bridge to an instrument involves more than carving the feet.

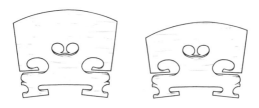

A blank bridge and one made to fit the instrument.

AND THE REST...

Violins and violas are fragile instruments that only give their best if everything is in place, nothing is loose and producing a buzz, and if nothing is worn out.

The sound post

If you have bought a new violin, it's a good idea to have it checked after six months or a year. One example of what an expert might spot is that the sound post may have become slightly too short as a result of the wood not having settled completely when you bought the instrument.

The tailpiece loop

Another example would be that the tailpiece loop may have stretched. If so, the distance between tailpiece and bridge will now be too short, which may muffle the sound. The correct distance is between about 2.2" and 2.4" (5.5– 6 cm) on a full-size violin, and about 2.75" on a viola. Adjustable tailpiece loops (also known as *tailpiece hangers* or *tail guts*) are available.

The fingerboard

However hard your fingerboard is, stopping the strings will wear grooves in it eventually, and your fingers will even create very shallow pits in the wood, especially if you perspire a lot. If you have a good, ebony fingerboard this is of course a very slow process. As an example, professional musicians, who play for many hours every day, often have their fingerboards reworked once a year or every two years. If your fingerboard has been reworked too often, you can have a new one fitted for around a hundred and fifty to two hundred and fifty dollars and up.

Loose pieces

If a piece of your violin breaks off, for instance along the edge, make sure that no moisture reaches that spot, and don't clean it. Take the instrument to a violin maker as soon as possible, and take the broken-off piece with you if you still have it. It's also best to see an expert if you find loose glue joints, or cracks. Tempted to glue them yourself? Don't.

Buzzes

A violin can start buzzing in all sorts of places. Some examples:
- The **nut or the saddle** may have come loose.
- If the bridge or the nut is **too low**, the strings may vibrate against the fingerboard.
- The **winding** of a string may be damaged.
- The **string ends** may vibrate if they are touching the pegbox or tailpiece.
- The **tailpiece** itself should not be touching the top or the chin rest at any point.

Purfling can work loose and cause buzzing.

- While checking the tailpiece, have a look at the **fine tuners** too.
- Is the **chin rest** securely fastened?
- Are the **sleeves** around the strings in the right place?
- A **wire mute** or loose **purfling** can also cause unwanted noises, and so can an **eye**, or a decorative **button** on a tuning peg, or a loose **glue joint**.
- … and there are other possible causes too…

DRY AIR

Wooden instruments are especially sensitive to dry air, and to rapid changes in humidity or temperature.

Freezing

Dry air is especially likely to be a problem if it is freezing outside and the central heating is on full blast. If humidity gets too low, the wood of your instrument will shrink. The result? If you're lucky, you'll only find that the string height is reduced, and that you need a winter bridge (see page 102). If you're less lucky, the tuning pegs may come loose—and it may get even worse: The top, the back or any other parts may crack.

Hygrometer

The best level of humidity, both for violins and for people, is often said to be around forty to sixty percent. A hygrometer is a device that allows you to keep an eye on the humidity level. You may have one in the room where you keep your violin, and some violin cases have one built-in. If the hygrometer shows that the air is getting too dry, it's time to do something about it.

Humidifiers

First, there are all kinds of small humidifiers that can be used inside the case, ranging from a very basic rubber tube with holes in it and a small sponge inside, to more complicated devices. Dampit is the best-known trade name. Prices are between about five and fifteen dollars, which sometimes includes a very basic humidity indicator. A stopgap solution would be to put a few slices of potato inside your case. Cases with a built-in hygrometer often feature a humidifier as well.

All-around solutions

If humidity is very low in your house, both your instrument and yourself (and wooden furniture and floors) may benefit from a central humidifier, if your heating system allows for one, or a portable one. Some examples of the latter are steam humidifiers (affordable, fast, but possibly noisy) and 'cold' humidifier systems which are quieter but more expensive, take longer to work, and may need more frequent maintenance.

Some time to adjust

Always give your instrument some time to adjust to changes in temperature and humidity. For example, if it's freezing cold outside and you enter a warm room, leave your instrument in its case for fifteen minutes, or as long as you can. The more gradually things change, the better your instrument will like it.

Heaters and vents

Some don'ts: Never store a violin in direct sunlight, or near heaters, fireplaces, air-conditioning vents, or anywhere else where it may get too hot, too dry, or too cold—not even if it's in its case.

ON THE ROAD

A few tips for when you travel with your violin:

- Make sure you have **a good case**, and check now and again to make sure that the handles and carrying straps are properly secured.
- In the car, your violin is safest **between the back and front seats**. The temperature is likely to be better there than in the trunk, and the chance of damage if you have an accident is smaller too. The worst place is under the rear window, especially on a sunny day, in full view of anyone who might fancy a violin.
- When you're in the train, tram, subway, or bus, keep your violin **on your lap**. It's safe, and you won't forget your instrument this way.
- Flying out? Carry your instrument as **hand luggage**.
- If you still leave your instrument behind somewhere, you're more likely to get it back if your **contact information** is listed inside your case.

Insurance

Consider insuring your instrument, especially if you're taking it on the road—which includes visiting your teacher. Musical instruments fall under the 'valuables' insurance category. A regular homeowner insurance policy will not cover all possible damage, whether it occurs at home, on the road, in the studio, or onstage. Companies that offer special insurances for musical instruments can be found in string players' magazines or on the Internet (see pages 129 –130). They may require you to have your instrument appraised before insuring it. Besides stating the value of the instrument, the appraisal report will also list various identifying features. You can list some of the essential data of your instrument yourself on pages 132–133. Final tip: Always check your insurance policy on the conditions for air travel.

12. BACK IN TIME

You could write hundreds of pages about the violin and its centuries-old history, and there are plenty of writers who have done just that. That's why the history chapter in this book has been kept nice and short.

People have written so much about the history of the violin because it's a fascinating story as well as a very long one, and also because there is a lot of disagreement about many of its facets. A few things are known for sure, though.

Bow and arrow

In the days when supper was still something you hunted, humans discovered that shooting an arrow produces a tone, due to the vibration of the bow's string.

The eighth century

The fact that you can also make a string vibrate by bowing it was only discovered much later. Exactly when is not certain, but bowed instruments were probably being played in ancient Persia, among other countries, as early as in the eighth century, and in Europe some time in the ninth century.

Fiddles

Apart from being used as a generic term for all bowed instruments, the word *fiddle* often refers to the instruments from the Middle Ages—and there were quite a few.

Lira da braccio

One of the best-known fiddles is the *lira da braccio*. Liras often had five or more strings, plus another two *bourdon strings* or *off-board drones*. These strings are not bowed or plucked, but they vibrate sympathetically with everything you play. The lira was played resting 'on the arm,' as the 'braccio' indicates: It's Italian for arm.

German viola

The lira da braccio is considered one of the predecessors of the violin and viola. Originally these instruments were played 'on the arm' as well, rather than held under the chin. Incidentally, the German word for viola, *Bratsche*, is derived from the Italian braccio.

Viola da gamba

Around the end of the fifteenth century, the first *viols* or *violas da gamba* were built. Contrary to the instruments da braccio, viols were played with the neck in an upright position. The smaller sizes were held with their tail on the knee of the musician; the larger ones were held between the legs ('gamba' is Italian for leg), like a cello.

Viola da gamba, a bowed instrument with frets and six strings.

The difference

Gambas are not just held differently, they also look different. For instance, they have sloped shoulders and more strings, and they have frets, just like guitars do. These ridges across the neck make it easier to play the instrument in tune: It is the exact position of the fret that produces the right pitch, rather than the exact position of your finger. On a gamba, the frets are gut strings that are wound around the neck. Gambas are tuned differently as well.

Amateurs and professionals

Another difference is that gambas or viols, with their delicate, soft sound, were mainly played by wealthy amateur musicians. Braccios or violins, by contrast, were especially popular with folk and dance musicians, who often earned their living by playing. With a violin on your arm you can dance and walk around as you play, and a violin produces more volume than a gamba, which is always useful at parties. Around two hundred years ago, the gambas gradually disappeared from the scene, and today they are rarely played.

The cello and the double bass

The cello is in fact a member of the braccio family, but because it is so big, it's played with its neck upright, the instrument standing between the legs of the musician. The double bass is a relative of both the braccios and the gambas. There's more about both instruments in the next chapter.

Amati and Stradivari

The first violins were built in the first half of the sixteenth century. One of those early violins, built by Andrea Amati, has even survived. Stradivarius made the violin's arch a little less pronounced around 1700, resulting in a stronger sound. This didn't gain him immediate popularity: People were used to the softer sound of violins with a higher arching. But in the years that followed, the demand for louder violins grew, especially because music was being performed in ever bigger halls.

From straight to curved

In that same period, the bow changed too. Curving the stick, which was originally straight, helped increase the volume potential of the instrument.

From gut to synthetic

The very first violins had non-wound gut strings. As early as the seventeenth century, it was discovered that the strings themselves could stay thinner if they were wound; the increased flexibility of thin, wound strings made them easier to play. The steel E-string became popular in the early 1900s, and the other steel strings followed some twenty years later. Synthetic-core strings came along in the 1950s.

13. THE FAMILY

The cello and the double bass are the two best-known relatives of the violin. But of course there are many more related instruments old and new, from the rabab to the kemenche and the Hardanger fele. The youngest relative—the electric violin—is covered in Chapter 9.

Violins and violas belong to the family of *string* or *stringed instruments*. They're also indicated as *bowed instruments*, which distinguishes them from plucked string instruments, such as guitars, banjos, and mandolins.

The cello

Tipcode VIOLIN-017

First the cello, which is not very different from the violin or the viola. The main difference is that it's quite a lot bigger. The four strings of the cello are tuned to the same notes as viola strings, only an octave lower (eight white keys on the piano). The instrument is often referred to using its original Italian name, violoncello, which literally means 'small, large violin.' Around 1700, Stradivarius built a cello which is still used as the standard model.

Double bass

The double bass looks like an even bigger violin, but actually there are quite a few differences. It is not so much a big brother as a distant cousin. Unlike a violin, the bass usually has sloped shoulders, and the back is often flat—though there are swelled-back versions too. The tuning is different as well, the strings being a fourth apart, rather than a fifth. They're tuned to E, A, D, G, from low to high, similar to a bass guitar. Another difference is that a double bass has tuning machines, rather than wooden tuning pegs. The double bass is often used outside classical music, in which case it is usually plucked instead of bowed—again, like a bass guitar.

Bourdon strings

Most of the other relatives are rare. The old *viola d'amore*, for instance; this is a kind of gamba with bourdon strings (see page 109) that is played like a violin. The Norwegian *Hardanger fele* is a smaller type of violin with four bourdon strings.

Rabab

There are many other bowed instruments with bourdon strings. The Afghan *rabab* or *rebab* shown below has twelve of them—but you may also come across rababs which have just two regular strings, and no bourdon strings at all. Just like other names, such as fiddle, the name rabab is used for a variety of bowed instruments.

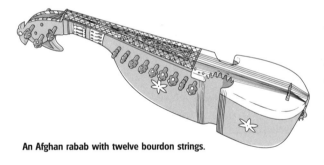

An Afghan rabab with twelve bourdon strings.

Pear-shaped or elongated

The same goes for the *kemenche*. This refers to a small, pear-shaped instrument with three strings used in Turkish classical music. But it can also indicate an elongated three-stringed instrument used to play folk music around the Black Sea and in Greece. The spelling varies as much as the shape, from *kemânje* to *kamaché*, and similar instruments can be referred to as rabab or rebabs as well. They're mostly played with their tail on the knee of the musician, with the neck held upright. You may even see musicians who play a regular violin that way. And *rebecs*? They come with two, three, or more strings, with various body shapes, with or without frets...

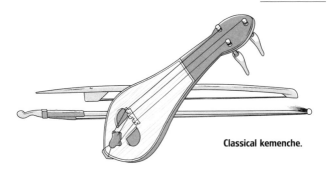

Classical kemenche.

With a fingernail

With some of these instruments, the different pitches are made not by stopping the strings on the fingerboard, but by touching them very lightly with a fingernail. The bow stick is often straight, and you tension the bow hair not with a frog but simply by wedging your fingers or a thumb between the stick and the hair.

Many more

Many other cultures have their own bowed instruments too, from the one-stringed Indian to tubular Native American models. The format of this book doesn't allow to list them all, but there are other books that do.

Ergonomic instruments

A violin is not the easiest instrument to hold, and a viola is even harder. As a result, violinists and violists often develop problems with their necks, arms, or fingers. To help prevent such symptoms, there are ergonomic instruments in various special designs.

An ergonomic violin: the Pelegrina (David Rivinus).

14. HOW THEY'RE MADE

Violins are still made in much the same way as they were hundreds of years ago, with chisels and files, with saws and planes, and with glue. Making a violin top in the traditional way may easily take a master violin maker a couple of days' work.

Tipcode VIOLIN-018

In a violin factory, machines are used for parts of the process, such as roughly shaping all the wooden components. Master violin makers who build an instrument by themselves from start to finish, still do everything by hand. Somewhere in between these two extremes are the workshops that buy unvarnished *white violins*, which are finished by hand and provided with fittings and strings.

Quarter-sawn wood is stronger that slab-cut wood.

Cake

The top and back are usually made of *quarter-sawn* or *quartered* wood—wood that has been sawed from the tree trunk in the shape of slices of cake. Each slice is then sawed almost in half to enhance the drying and seasoning process of the wood, which will make it less likely to warp, split, or shrink later on.

Bookmatched

This slice is later sawed through completely to make two separate halves. These halves are folded open, like a book, and then glued with their backs together. The result is the beginning of a *bookmatched plate*, the two halves being each other's mirror images. Not all plates are bookmatched.

Carved

Traditionally, the top and the back are then carved into shape. Using dies and thickness gauges (graduation calipers), and simply by feel, the violin maker keeps checking to see if any more wood needs to be removed. The exact graduation is essential for the performance of the instrument.

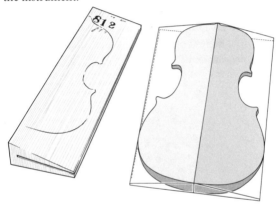

Folded open like a book, then glued together.

The ribs

The ribs of the instrument are moistened so they can be shaped, and glued to the top, bottom, and corner blocks that strengthen them at the joints. The rib structure is

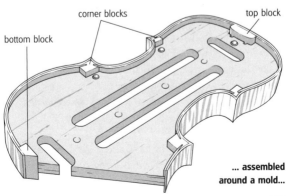

corner blocks

top block

bottom block

... assembled around a mold...

assembled around a mold, which is of course later removed. The willow or spruce lining adds strength to the instrument, and the same strips of wood are necessary to glue the plates to the ribs.

Cut by hand
The *f*-holes and the channel for the purfling are traditionally cut by hand. Making the bass bar also takes a long time, as it has to be made to fit the inside arch of the top exactly.

Jigsaw puzzle
The neck and scroll are carved from a single block of wood. The neck slots into the top block like a piece in a jigsaw puzzle. The weight of the fingerboard, which is made of heavy ebony, is reduced by hollowing out the underside.

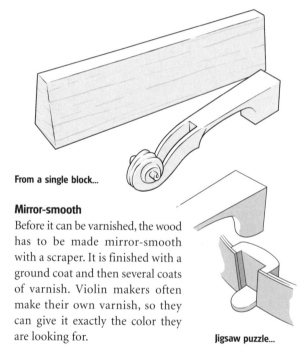

From a single block...

Mirror-smooth
Before it can be varnished, the wood has to be made mirror-smooth with a scraper. It is finished with a ground coat and then several coats of varnish. Violin makers often make their own varnish, so they can give it exactly the color they are looking for.

Jigsaw puzzle...

Bows
The bow stick is first cut by hand and shaped over a flame. The horsehair is held in place in the frog and head by small wooden wedges.

Wonderful stories

There are lots of wonderful stories told about the secret of those expensive old Italian violins. For instance, it is said that the wood used to make them was transported by dragging it behind a sailing ship, and that it is the salt sea water that gives the violins their special sound. Others say that the wood comes from centuries-old church towers which burned down; the wood was first broken in by vibrations from the church bells and then ripened by the fire... Or perhaps the varnish is the greatest 'secret' of those old violins—and the secret is safe, because the materials that were used back then are no longer available today.

15. VIOLIN BRANDS AND MAKERS

When you go out to buy a violin or a viola, you'll come across dozens of brand names—names of violin makers young, old, or dead, names of violin makers who never even lived, brand names and names of towns, and regions. This chapter sheds some light on the violin and viola market, and it introduces you to some of the old masters.

When you go shopping for a violin, you're bound to come across dozens of German names: Germany has always had a great reputation for producing good instruments in every price range. As a result, many violins bear a German name, even though they have been made elsewhere, either in Europe or in Asia. Italian names are popular too, based on the rich violin heritage of this country. And as Chinese instruments have improved over the years, Chinese brand names have become well accepted.

Brand names

A certain brand name may be given to violins made by various different workshops or factories—or a single brand name may be used for instruments with components from three different countries, which are assembled in a fourth country, varnished in a fifth, and shop-adjusted by the distributor or dealer. So brand names on violins do not always tell you much about the instrument's origins.

Quality

On the other hand, of course, there are many companies that sell good, adjusted instruments only, and their (brand) names can be seen as a guarantee for a certain quality. Some examples would be **Otto Brückner**, **F. Cervini**, **Glaesel**, **Knilling**, **Mathias Thoma**, **Meisel**, **Palatino**, **Scherl & Roth**, and **Wm. Lewis & Son**, and other names which are listed in this chapter. Do note that this chapter is not intended to be complete, and that brand names may have been discontinued, sold, or changed by the time you read this.

Germany

The German towns of Bubenreuth, Mittenwald, Klingenthal, and Markneukirchen are famous for their violin-making traditions and for the instruments made there today. A good, hundred-year-old factory violin from any of these places easily costs between a thousand to fifteen hundred dollars or more. A few of today's better-known names are **Götz**, **Höfner**, **Paesold**, and **Stein**.

Eastern Europe

Many of the founders of German violin companies came from the Czech city of Luby, which is often referred to as the 'Czech Mittenwald.' Other Eastern European countries, such as Hungary, Romania, and Bulgaria also have long violin-making traditions, from master instruments to low-priced factory-made student violins. Some names include **Dvorak**, **Lidl**, and **Strunal** (Czech Republic), **Grygo Petrof** (Bulgaria), and **Bucharest** and **Vasile Gliga** (Romania). The Romanian center of violin making is Reghin.

Asia

String instruments from China, Korea and other Asian countries used to have a poor reputation, but their quality has improved over the years—Chinese instruments especially. Some examples of better-known Chinese companies would include **Ren Wei Shi**, **Samuel Shen**, and **Xue Chang Sun**. Still, most Asian-made instruments can be found in the lower price ranges. German wood may be used for more expensive models. **Nagoya Suzuki** is one of the better-known Japanese brands, mainly known for their smaller violins.

France

France no longer produces large numbers of violins, but two hundred years ago the French town of Mirecourt was home to the world's first real violin factory, employing some six hundred people. The prices of old French factory-made instruments are usually a little higher than those of comparable German violins. The French violins sound a little louder and brighter than the German ones, some say – and others claim to hear the opposite.

Other countries

In most countries you'll be able to find master violin makers who make high-quality instruments entirely by hand, usually to order. Most of them also sell used instruments, bows, and accessories, and they repair and rebuild instruments too.

(Master) violin makers

Not everybody who uses the name 'violin maker' is a *master* violin maker. Some mainly do repairs of student and intermediate violins, or they specialize in expensive instruments only; others concentrate on finishing and setting up white violins (see page 114), and so on. The exact number of master violin makers is unknown, but there must be over a hundred of them in the US alone. Most countries have an association or federation of violin and bow makers, which you'll be able to trace on the Internet or in string players' magazines (see pages 129–130).

OLD MASTERS

Many books list the stories of dozens or even hundreds of violin makers from the past, where and when they lived and worked, and what their instruments could be worth today. Still, there's a good chance that the maker of your old violin won't be mentioned, simply because there are too many of them. Here's a very short introduction to some of the most famous names.

Italy

The most famous Italian violins were built in the town of Cremona, from the sixteenth century onwards. **Andrea Amati** (1525-1611) was one of the first violin makers. His grandson **Nicolo Amati** taught the craft to **Francesco Ruggieri** (1620-c.1695), the most famous member of another important Cremonese violin-making family.

Another of Nicolo's pupils was **Antonio Stradivari** (often referred to as Stradivarius), who lived from 1644 to 1737. Apart from violins and cellos, Stradivarius also made harps and guitars. Of his bowed instruments, around six hundred have survived. **Carlo Bergonzi** and **Joseph Guarnerius del Gesu** (1698–1744), the best-known member of the Guarnerius family, were among Stradivarius' pupils.

Outside Cremona

Apart from the Cremonese school or style, to which all of these violin makers belonged, there were also Venetian, Milanese, and other schools. Each school of makers had its own characteristics, such as the shape of the *f*-holes and the precise model of the body. Experts can often tell a master violin's maker by simply looking at the scroll.

Germany

Jacob Stainer, who died in 1683, is often seen as the founder of German violin-making. Until well into the eighteenth century, a violin made by Stainer was more expensive than a Stradivarius; the latter was often considered 'too loud.' **Mathias Klotz I** (1656–1743), who was very important for violin-making in Mittenwald, studied under Stainer and Nicolo Amati. Instruments made by the slightly younger **Sebastian Klotz** are still highly prized. One of the major violin-making families in the German town of Klingenthal was **Hopf**, including Caspar (1650–1711) and his grandson David.

France

Two important French violin masters were **Nicolas Lupot** (1758–1824) and, from Mirecourt, **Jean Baptiste Vuillaume** (1798–1875).

England

The best-known English violin name is **Hill**. Hill's bows are still famous, and you often find the description 'Hill model' on tailpieces, tuning pegs, and other parts.

The Netherlands

Violins made by the Dutch luthiers **Hendrik Jacobs** (1630–1704) and **Johannes Cuypers** (1766–1828) are usually valued at about twenty-five to fifty thousand dollars.

GLOSSARY AND INDEX

This glossary contains short definitions of all the violin-related words used in this book. There are also some words you won't find in the previous pages, but which you might well come across in magazines, catalogs, and on the Internet. The numbers refer to the pages where the terms are used in this book.

Adjuster See: *Fine tuners* and *Screw button*.

Antiquing *(27)* Technique to make violins look older than they are.

Back, back plate See: *Flamed wood* and *Top*.

Baroque violin *(34)* Special, mellow sounding gut-stringed violin to play the music of the Baroque era.

Bass bar *(9, 10)* Wooden bar on the inside of the top.

Belly See: *Top*.

Body *(5, 6, 29–32)* The body consists of the top, the back, and the sides.

Bottom nut See: *Saddle*.

Bow *(10–11, 57–64, 94–96)* Violins and violas are played with a bow. The bow is very important for the sound of the instrument. See also: *Bow hair*, *Frog*, and *Stick*.

Bow grip *(11, 60)* Piece of (synthetic) leather wrapped around the stick of the bow; also refers to the (silver, silk or imitation baleen) *winding* or *lapping* next to it; a.k.a. *thumb grip*.

Bow hair *(58, 94–96)* The hair of the bow; either horsehair or synthetic. Also know as *ribbon*.

Bridge *(6, 7, 35–37, 101–103)* The strings run over

the bridge, which passes the vibrations of the strings on to the top.

Button See: *End button.*

Catgut The oldest material used for violin strings. The name comes from *cattle gut*, although actually sheep gut is used.

C-bout *(6)* The waist of the body.

Cello *(2, 4, 110, 111)* Another bowed, string(ed) instrument. Sounds an octave lower than a viola.

Channel *(6, 8, 31)* The 'valley' near the edge of both the top and the back before the upward arching begins.

Cheeks *(6, 47)* The sides of the pegbox.

Children's violins *(12–13, 56)* See: *Fractional sizes.*

Chin rest *(6, 8, 68–71)* The chin rest sits beside or above the tailpiece.

Curl See: *Flamed wood.*

Double bass *(2, 110, 111–112)* The lowest-sounding string instrument.

Ebony See: *Wood.*

Electric violin *(17, 80–84)* An electric violin can be plugged straight into an amplifier, just like an electric guitar.

End button *(7)* The tailpiece is attached to the end button or *button*, which is also known as *end pin*.

End pin See: *End button.*

End screw See: *Screw button.*

Eye, Parisian eye *(39, 59)* Inlaid decoration on tuning pegs, frogs, and other parts. A Parisian eye is a mother-of-pearl dot with a small metal ring around it.

ƒ-hole *(5, 6, 121)* The soundholes of a violin are shaped like an *f.*

Figured wood See: *Flamed wood.*

Fine tuners *(7, 39–40, 54, 85, 87, 89)* Small, additional tuning mechanisms in the tailpiece. Also referred to as *tuning adjusters*, *string tuners*, and *string adjusters.*

Fingerboard *(6, 7, 32–33, 103–104)* When you play, you press down or *stop* the strings against the fingerboard.

123

Tailpiece with adjustable loop and built-in fine tuners.

Fittings Collective name for the violin's replaceable parts, *e.g.*, tailpiece, pegs, and nut, but the fingerboard as well. Also known as the *trim*.

Flamed wood *(28)* Many violins have a back and ribs which look as though they have been 'licked by flames.' This *flamed*, *figured*, or *curled* wood is usually more expensive than *plain wood*.

Fractional sizes *(12–13)* Violins and violas in small or *proportional* sizes, designed for children. Fractional-sized instruments require fractional-sized strings *(56)* and bows *(59)*.

Frog *(58, 59)* One end of the bow hair is held in place inside the frog. At the bottom of the frog is the *slide*. Most frogs are *full-lined* with a metal *back plate*. At the front, where the hair enters the frog, it passes through the *ferrule* or *D-ring*.

F-stop See: *String length.*

Full-size violin *(12–13)* The regular, 4/4 size violin. See also: *Fractional sizes.*

Fully-carved *(115)* Fully-carved instruments have tops and backs made by carving only.

German silver See: *Nickel silver.*

Hair See: *Bow hair.*

Heel *(8)* Semi-circular projection of the back.

Insurance *(107, 132–133)* A good idea.

Lining *(116)* Thin strips of wood glued to the inside edges of the body.

Luthier Another name for a (master) violin maker.

Master violin *(21–22)* Built by a master violin maker from start to finish.

Mensur ratio See: *String length.*

Mountings *(58)* The metal parts of a bow.

Mute *(16, 74–76)* A mute makes your sound a little sweeter and softer. *Practice mutes* muffle the sound a lot.

Neck *(6, 7, 33–34)* The long wooden section that extends from the instrument's body. The fingerboard is attached to the neck.

Nickel silver *(58)* Mixture of copper, zinc, and nickel. Also known as *alpaca* and *German silver*.

Nut *(6, 7, 32–33)* The wooden strip over which the strings run at the top end of the neck. Also called *top nut*.

Parisian eye See: *Eye, Parisian eye*.

Peg, pegbox *(5, 6)* The (tuning) pegs are fitted into the pegbox. See also: *Tuning pegs*.

Peg compound, peg dope *(94)* Lubricant for tuning pegs.

Pegging The process of fitting the tuning pegs to the instrument.

Pickup *(80–82)* Small, thin sensor that converts the vibrations of your strings into electrical signals, so that you can plug your violin into an amplifier.

Plain strings *(50)* Unwound strings. See also: *Wound strings*.

Plain wood See: *Flamed wood*.

Plates The back and the top or table of the instrument.

Pochette Violin with a very slim body; popular from the sixteenth well into the eighteenth century.

Practice mute See: *Mute*.

Practice violin *(17)* A violin without a soundbox for silent practice.

Proportional instruments See: *Fractional sizes*.

Purfling *(6, 8, 29)* Inlaid decoration; also protects the top and back.

Quarter-cut, quarter-sawn wood *(114)* If you saw a tree trunk or sections of it into quarters (the way you would cut a cake into slices), you get stronger wood than if you *slab-cut* the tree. Because quarter-sawn wood is stronger, it is good for making thin yet strong tops and backs.

Ribbon See: *Bow hair.*

Ribs *(31–32)* The sides of the body.

Rosin *(11, 64–67, 94–96)* Without rosin to make the bow hair sticky, your bow will do nothing at all.

Saddle *(6, 8)* A strip, usually of ebony, that prevents the top from being damaged by the loop that holds the tailpiece in place. Also known as *bottom nut.*

Screw button *(10, 11, 58)* Used to tighten and relax the bow hair. Also called *end screw* or *adjuster.*

Scroll *(5, 6, 28, 121)* The scroll or *volute* is the decoration at the top of the neck. Often referred to as the *maker's signature.*

Shoulder rest *(8, 71–73)* Ranging from simple pads or cushions to complicated, multi-adjustable supports.

Sleeves *(55, 100)* Protect the bridge from the strings, and the other way around.

Slide See: *Frog.*

Sound post *(9, 10, 37)* Thin, round piece of wood wedged between top and

back. Referred to as the 'soul' of the violin.

Stick *(10, 11, 57–58)* The wooden – or synthetic – part of your bow.

Stop See: *String length.*

Stradivarius *(23, 30, 121)* Antonio Stradivari, often referred to as Stradivarius, is the world's most famous violin-maker. He also built the standard model for the cello.

String adjusters See: *Fine tuners.*

String height *(34–35, 102)* The distance from the strings to the fingerboard, measured at the end nearest the bridge.

String length *(13, 29)* Usually refers to the length of the strings between nut and bridge, also known as their *speaking length.* Violin makers also use the term *f-stop,* referring to the distance from the top edge of the body to the notches of the *f*-holes. The ratio between the distance from the nut to the edge, and from the edge to the notches is referred to as the *stop* or the *mensur ratio.* In violins that ratio is usually 2:3 (13:19.5 cm, equaling

5.12":7.48"). String length is also referred to as *scale*.

String tuners See: *Fine tuners*.

Strings *(11–12, 48–56)*, **replacing strings** *(96–101)* Violin strings are available in gut, synthetic-core, and steel-core versions, and with windings made of all kinds of metals.

Table See: *Top*.

Tailgut See: *Tailpiece, tailpiece loop*.

Tailpiece, tailpiece loop *(6, 7, 41–42)* The strings are attached to the tailpiece, and the tailpiece is attached to the end button with the tailpiece loop or *tailgut (103)*.

Top *(5, 6, 30–31)* One of the most important components of a violin: the top of the body, also known as *table* or *belly*. The opposite side is the *back*.

Top nut See: *Nut*.

Trim See: *Fittings*.

Tuning *(38–41, 85–90)* Violins are tuned using the tuning pegs or the fine tuners.

Tuning adjusters See: *Fine tuners*.

Tuning pegs *(5, 6, 38–41, 93–94)* Violins have a tuning peg (often simply called peg) for each string, sometimes in combination with a fine tuner. The peg head is known as the *thumb piece*. See also: *Fine tuners*.

Varnish *(26–27, 117)* The varnish used is important for the sound and the appearance of your violin, and for the way you need to clean it.

Volute See: *Scroll*.

White violins *(114)* Unfinished violins.

Winding See: *Bow grip and Wound strings*.

Wolf tone, wolf tone eliminator *(76)* A wolf tone is a stuttering effect which is quite rare in violins but less so in cellos. Wolf tones can be cured using a wolf tone eliminator.

Wound strings *(49)* Most violin strings are wound with metal wire; often the E-string is the only unwound or plain string.

TIPCODE LIST

The Tipcodes in this book offer easy access to short movies, photo series, soundtracks, and other additional information at www.tipbook.com. For your convenience, the Tipcodes in this Tipbook have been listed below.

Tipcode	Topic	Chapter	Pages
VIOLIN-001	Violin and viola	**1**	1
VIOLIN-002	Various styles	**1**	1
VIOLIN-003	Stopping the strings	**2**	7
VIOLIN-004	Pizzicato	**3**	14
VIOLIN-005	Practice mute	**3**	16
VIOLIN-006	Fine tuners	**5, 10**	39, 87
VIOLIN-007	Spiccato	**7**	62
VIOLIN-008	Tuning pegs	**10**	85, 90
VIOLIN-009	Tuning fork	**10**	87
VIOLIN-010	Fifths	**10**	88
VIOLIN-011	String pitches violin	**10**	88
VIOLIN-012	String pitches viola	**10**	88
VIOLIN-013	Adjacent strings	**10**	88
VIOLIN-014	Applying rosin	**11**	94
VIOLIN-015	Removing strings	**11**	97
VIOLIN-016	Fitting strings	**11**	98
VIOLIN-017	Cello and double bass	**13**	111
VIOLIN-018	Violin maker at work	**14**	114

WANT TO KNOW MORE?

Tipbooks supply you with basic information on the instrument of your choice, and everything that has to do with it. Of course, there's a lot more to be found on all subjects you came across on the previous pages. A selection of magazines, books and websites, as well as some information on the makers of the Tipbook series.

MAGAZINES
- *STRINGS*, phone (415) 485-6946, subs.st@stringletter.com, www.stringsmagazine.com.
- *The Strad* (UK), www.thestrad.com.
- *The Journal of the Violin Society of America*, phone (845) 452-7557, www.vsa.to (see page 130).
- *Journal of the American Viola Society*, phone (972) 233 9107, www.americanviolasociety.org/
- *AST Journal, Journal of the American String Teachers Association*, phone (703) 279 2113, www.astaweb.com.
- *Stringendo, Journal of the Australian Strings Association*, phone +61 3 9376 1506, www.austa.asn.au/journal.html.
- *American Lutherie*, phone (253) 472 7853, www.luth.org (stringed instrument making and repair; covers guitars and other fretted instruments as well).

BOOKS
There are dozens of books on violins and violas. The following is a brief selection of publications that cover some of the subjects of this Tipbook in greater depth.
- *Cambridge Companion to the Violin*, Robin Stowell (Cambridge University Press, 1992/1998; 303 pages; ISBN 0 521 39923 8).

- *The Violin Explained – Components, Mechanism and Sound*, James Beament (Clarendon Press, England, 1997; 245 pages; ISBN 0 1 981 6623 0).
- *Violin and Viola*, Yehudi Menuhin and William Primrose (Kahn & Averill, 1991; 250 pages; ISBN 1 871 08219 6).
- *The Amadeus Book of the Violin: Construction, History, and Music,* by Walter Kolneder, Reinhard G. Pauly (Translator) (Amadeus Press, 1998; 600 pages; ISBN 1 574 67038 7).
- *Violin Owner's Manual: The Complete Guide,* Heather Scott (String Letter Publishing, 2001; 158 pages; ISBN 1 890490 43 1).

Special editions

There are also very specialized – usually quite expensive – books, often in a very limited edition only, which may be of interest if you really want to go in-depth. Some examples would be *Violin Restoration – A Manual for Violin Makers,* by Hans Weisshaar and Margaret Shipman (1988; ISBN 0 962 18610 4); or one of the books that deal with the violin makers of a specific country only, such as *400 Years of Violin Making in The Netherlands* (1999; limited edition); or *The Violin Book – A Complete History* (Miller Freeman Books, 1999; limited edition).

INTERNET

On the Internet, you'll find countless sites for violinists, often with all kinds of links, articles, discussion groups, and FAQ's (Frequently Asked Questions – and their answers). Following are some good starting points:

- www.maestronet.com
- members.aol.com/FiddleNet
- www.viola.com (The Viola website)
- www.JazzStringCaucus.org (growth and development of string jazz and jazz education)
- www.phys.unsw.edu.au/music/violin (Violin Acoustics)
- www.violintips.com

Smithsonian Institution

Of course, you can also check out whether there is anything on the maker of your violin by searching the Internet under that name. If you are interested in the great old masters, take a look at The Smithsonian Institution's site at www.si.edu/resource/faq/nmah/violins.htm.

VIOLIN SOCIETY OF AMERICA

The Violin Society Of America (VSA; 1974) promotes the art and science of making, repairing, and preserving the instruments and bows of the violin family. The VSA organizes an annual convention featuring speakers, demonstrations of violin and bow making and repair, performances, and more. For more information call (845)452-7557 or visit www.vsa.to. The VSA also publishes a journal and a quarterly newsletter.

ORGANIZATIONS

Following are some other organizations for string players and string teachers; the latter can be of help in finding a teacher in your area.

- American String Teachers Association: www.astaweb.com
- European String Teachers Association, British Branch: www.estaweb.org.uk
- Australian Strings Association: www.austa.asn.au/home.html.
- The Canadian Viola Society: www.viola.ca
- The American Viola Society www.americanviola-society.org/
- American Federation of Violin and Bow Makers: www.afvbm.com
- British Violin Making Association: www.bvma.org.uk/ index.htm

THE TIPBOOK SERIES

Tipbook Violin and Viola is just one of the successful volumes of the Tipbook Series. One of the other Tipbooks that you may find of interest is *Tipbook Music on Paper*, a handy reference on music theory. This books starts at the very beginning, and includes almost all signs and symbols you can come across when reading music, as well as the system behind the notes. Special feature: Most musical examples in the book can be heard at www.tipbook.com, using our unique Tipcodes! *Tipbook Music on Paper* is used by both beginners and advanced musicians in all styles of music.

Do you play an electric violin, or would you like to know more about amplification and effects? Check out *Tipbook Amplifiers & Effects*!

All current Tipbooks are shown on page 134. Please visit www.tipbook.com for additional and up-to-date information.

ESSENTIAL DATA

In the event of your instrument being stolen or lost, or if you decide to sell it, it's useful to have all the relevant data at hand. Here are two pages to make those notes. For the insurance, for the police, or just for yourself. There's also room to list the strings you're currently using, for future reference.

INSURANCE

Company:

Phone: Email:

Agent:

Phone: Email:

Policy number:

Insured amount: Premium:

VIOLIN

You'll find some of the details of your violin on the label, which – if there is one at all – is usually visible through the *f*-hole on the side of the G or C-string. Some violins have labels which you can only read if the body is opened. The name of the maker can also be branded in the body, for example on the back, close to the heel.

Make and model:

Manufacturer/violin maker:

Serial number:

Color:

Make of bridge:

Tailpiece	Make:
	Type:
	Color/material:
Chin rest	Make:
	Type:
	Color/material:
Shoulder rest	Make:
	Type:
	Color/material:

Description of tuning pegs:

Any repairs, damage or other distinguishing features:

Date of purchase: Price:

Place of purchase:

Phone: Email:

W

Name/maker:

                                     Price:

Octagonal/round:

Fitting:

Place of purchase:

Date of purchase:

                                     Email:

GS

List the strings you're currently using, you'll later be able to buy the
same ones if you like them, or different ones if you don't.

Violin/viola	Make	Type	Gauge/tension	Date
E/A				
A/D				
D/G				
G/C				
A				
D				
G				

133